A LESSON IN LOVE

What does intelligence have to do with love? Most people believe the two exist in separate realms. Love is intuitive and emotional; intelligence is rational and deliberative. We *fall* in love. We *decide* on a career. This belief leads many of us to a point of resignation. We accept the fact that we behave in foolish and even self-destructive ways when we're in the grip of love. We resist the idea that we might be able to learn to be more effective in our relationships. It seems too contrived. We're afraid that if we approach relationships in a strategic way, they'll lose their romantic edge.

If you're like most people, when your relationships fail, you are filled with guilt and self-recrimination. You believe that you should have known how to make things work. But why should you have known? Where have you learned to be smart in your relationships?

What you will learn by reading this book is that there is such a thing as Relationship Intelligence (R.I.). I am going to teach you how you can be effective, happy, and fulfilled in your relationships by applying new techniques that you never learned in school or on the job.

LOVE
THE WAY YOU
WANT IT

USING YOUR HEAD
IN MATTERS OF THE HEART

❖

Dr. Robert J. Sternberg

WITH

Catherine Whitney

BANTAM

NEW YORK   TORONTO   LONDON   SYDNEY   AUCKLAND

LOVE THE WAY YOU WANT IT
A Bantam Nonfiction Book / March 1991

PUBLISHING HISTORY
Bantam hardcover edition published March 1991
Bantam paperback edition / August 1992

*BANTAM NONFICTION and the portrayal of a boxed "b" are
trademarks of Bantam Books, a division of Bantam Doubleday Dell
Publishing Group, Inc.*

ISBN 0-553-29788-0

Published simultaneously in the United States and Canada

*Bantam Books are published by Bantam Books, a division of Bantam Doubleday
Dell Publishing Group, Inc. Its trademark, consisting of the words "Bantam Books"
and the portrayal of a rooster, is Registered in U.S. Patent and Trademark Office
and in other countries. Marca Registrada. Bantam Books, 666 Fifth Avenue, New
York, New York 10103.*

PRINTED IN THE UNITED STATES OF AMERICA
RAD   0 9 8 7 6 5 4 3 2 1

This book is dedicated to

Ellen Berscheid and Elaine Hatfield,
who have helped to make the study of love
a respectable scientific endeavor, and who have given
generously of themselves, personally and professionally.

ACKNOWLEDGMENTS

I would like to thank Catherine Whitney for making my ideas intelligible to the readers of this book. I would also like to thank my editors, Alexandra Penney and Barbara Alpert, for all of their help in bringing the book to fruition. Thanks also to my agent, John Brockman, who helped me find a good home for the book. Finally, I would like to thank all those in my life who have taught me about "Love the Way You Want It."

CONTENTS

PART ONE

CRAZY
IN LOVE

BLOCKING OUT YOUR SMART
RESPONSES

I always cringe a little when I am called an "intelligence expert," since it implies that I'm something of a know-it-all. But I have struggled as deeply as anyone with the question that seems to be most on people's minds, and that is, what is the relationship between love and intelligence? Put more practically, the question often gets asked this way: "Why am I so smart in my work and so dumb in my personal relationships?" or "If I have such a high I.Q., why is my love life in such lousy shape?" I finally decided to study love and intelligence during a period when my own personal life was in disarray. The study was more than academic. It seemed to me that there must be a better way to approach interpersonal relationships. Literally, a *smarter* way.

When I wrote *The Triangle of Love,* it was an attempt to identify the components of love—to take love apart and view it from the inside out. But I knew that understanding is only one part of knowledge. The next step is to apply that knowledge to the practical domains of life. This book is the result of my exploration of how the equation worked.

What does intelligence have to do with love? Most people believe the two exist in separate realms. Love is intuitive and emotional; intelligence is rational and deliberative. We *fall* in love. We *decide* on a career. This belief leads many of us to a point of resignation. We accept the fact that we behave in foolish and even self-destructive ways when we're in the grip of love. We resist the idea that we might be able to learn to be

3

more effective in our relationships. It seems too contrived. We're afraid that if we approach relationships in a strategic way, they'll lose their romantic edge.

If you're like most people, when your relationships fail, you are filled with guilt and self-recrimination. You believe that you should have known how to make things work. But why should you have known? Where have you learned to be smart in your relationships?

What you will learn by reading this book is that there is such a thing as Relationship Intelligence (R.I.). I am going to teach you how you can be effective, happy, and fulfilled in your relationships by applying new techniques that you never learned in school or on the job.

The absence of R.I. makes you susceptible to a whole series of romantic myths that you hang onto for dear life, believing that they will make love work. Once you learn the techniques of R.I., you will understand more clearly how empty of substance these myths really are. And you will see why the kind of intelligence that serves you so well in other arenas of your life does not work when you try to apply it to love.

CHAPTER ONE

FOOLED BY LOVE

THE MYTH OF THE IDEAL
RELATIONSHIP

Do you look at your love life and find yourself asking:

- How did I ever get into this relationship?
- Why am I still in this relationship?
- How could I have lost him/her?
- Why do I keep making the same mistakes over and over again with him/her?
- Why do we keep talking past each other instead of talking to each other?
- Why can't I figure out what is wrong with this relationship?
- Why can't I get him/her to change?

If you are like most people, you're no stranger to some or all of these questions. No matter how intelligent, competent, or skillful you are in other domains, you may find yourself repeatedly frustrated when you try to transfer these abilities to the art of loving.

This dilemma causes great pain for many people. Every year, millions of men and women flock to the bookstores or tune into popular television talk shows looking for some insight into why they can't make their relationships work. They're seeking a new key to unlock the mystery, but they often walk away feeling dissatisfied. In fact, the popular wisdom about achieving success in love hasn't changed much over the years, in spite of the careful examination it has received in the media. We may be more aggressive about looking for solutions than were previous generations, but most of us basically trust the old wisdom without really questioning its validity. When our relationships fail, we blame ourselves. It rarely occurs to us that we should question our fundamental assumptions.

Although certain ideas about love are commonly accepted as fact, scientific research on relationships has shown each of them to be flawed. We get into trouble in our relationships when we measure our reality against these myths—saying, for example, "If he loved me, he wouldn't . . ." or "I thought people who loved each other were supposed to . . ." As the gap between our culturally inspired expectations and our actual circumstances widens, we assume that something is wrong with us.

We readily accept these myths about relationships because they seem to supply the "markers" we need as we travel the uncertain paths of love. No other arena of our lives seems filled with the same degree of confusion and ambiguity; in no other arena are we so consistently at a loss for solutions. In the absence of guidelines, we place our trust in popular assumptions, even when they do not seem consistent with our experiences. Our literature is filled with "answers" that let us off the hook or, conversely, fill us with guilt.

The first step in developing Relationship Intelligence is to see why the common myths of love are not true. There are many such myths; people live them out every day. I have chosen ten very common myths to illustrate the chasm that often exists between our love ideology and our real lives.

MYTH #1

The best predictor of happiness in a relationship is how deeply you feel about each other.

When Michael Barnes, a graduate student at Yale, and I studied what predicts success in relationships, we found that, contrary to popular belief, the best predictor is not how deeply you feel about one another. Rather, success in relationships is measured by the difference between the way you would ideally like your partner to feel about you and the way you actually perceive your partner to feel. Simply put, it is the difference between what you think you want and what you think you are getting.

Jason and Cynthia have been dating for three months, but Jason feels constantly on guard because he's afraid that Cynthia is pushing for an early commitment. That's the last thing he wants right now, having ended a seven-year marriage just two years ago. His feelings for Cynthia are strong, but he thinks he needs more time before he settles down again.

Why does Jason think Cynthia wants to force a commitment he's not ready for? He has trouble putting his finger on it, but there are a number of signs: The way

she asks so many questions and seems overly interested in the answers; the concern he glimpses when he
mentions going out with other women; the way she's so
solicitous of him; the way she gets so emotional about
things he says and does.

If you were to ask Cynthia for her perspective on the
relationship, she would say, "There's such a bond between us. I feel as though we were meant to be together." It bothers Cynthia that Jason sometimes
seems withdrawn, but she is counting on that to change
with time. And there will be time; Cynthia expects them
to be together forever.

Clearly, there is a tremendous gap between the way
Jason and Cynthia perceive the future of their relationship. But consider a different scenario. What if Cynthia
and Jason both felt deeply in love, and could hardly wait
for every moment they would be together? What if Jason were as passionately involved in the relationship as
Cynthia? Even if they shared this depth of feeling, it
would not necessarily tell them very much about their
overall prospects as a couple. Jason might *feel* filled
with love for Cynthia, but still be unwilling to make a
commitment. His perception of what his feelings mean
might be quite different from Cynthia's.*

Perhaps the greatest myth of love is that the more
deeply it is felt, the more "true" it is—and therefore,
the more likely there is to be a successful love match.
But when you fail to make the connection between your
feelings and your perceptions, you are often left wondering why the most promising relationships don't
work out.

In matters of love, we tend to place an overwhelming

* The examples in this book are drawn from actual experiences. To
protect the privacy of the individuals who told me about their relationships, however, names and other identifying details have been
changed.

trust in feelings: a quickening heartbeat, sweaty palms, the dizzying sensations of desire and passion. When these feelings are present, they stand as proof that we are legitimately "in love." But feelings provide a shaky basis for drawing conclusions about the potential of relationships. If our perceptions and expectations are mismatched, all the feelings in the world won't change that fact.

MYTH #2

Living together before marriage will demonstrate whether you will succeed together once you are married.

Nick and Charlene lived together for almost three years before they got married. Both had successful careers—Nick as a lawyer and Charlene as the buyer for a major department store chain. During the time they lived together, they were both satisfied with the arrangement. Each felt available for the other, but they avoided stepping on each other's toes. They were convinced they were right for each other and they got married.

Charlene's disappointment began only a few months after the wedding. Nick seemed to have changed. At first, the changes were slight but, as time went on, he seemed to grow more and more restless. When they argued, Nick often accused Charlene of trying to hold him back, and this attitude confused her because their relationship had always been one of equal sharing—interdependent, rather than dependent.

Charlene also felt Nick was backing down on some of the important agreements they had made before they were married, such as having children and buying a house. He said they weren't ready to make such big commitments, but Charlene wondered how they could not be ready. They had lived together for three years before marriage. She thought getting married was a sign that they *were* ready for the big commitments.

How could Nick and Charlene have such separate views of their relationship after they had lived together for three years?

Actually, people who live together before marriage are statistically more likely to get divorced than people who do not live together before marriage. Yet, the living together was supposed to be a test of how the couple would function together. Why doesn't it necessarily work? It's probably a combination of several factors.

First, people who live together before marriage are likely to be more shy of commitment than those who do not. By living together first, they hope to convince themselves beyond any reasonable doubt that things will work out in the long run. But once they are married, they often continue to be shy of commitment. They still test their partners as they did before the marriage. As they discover the seriousness of the commitment they have made, they may find it hard to accept what they have done, especially when things get difficult. And at some point, things do get difficult in *any* marriage.

A second explanation of why people who live together first are more likely to have trouble after marriage has to do with a psychological condition called "reactance." Reactance is rebellion against a perceived threat to freedom. We sometimes call it the "trapped wolf" syndrome. People differ in how prone they are to reactance, just as their reactions would differ if they were actually caged in a prison or under house arrest. People who live together before marriage may be more susceptible to reactance. In fact, this disposition might be part of what led them to live together in the first place, since living together left them the option of walking away if they started to feel trapped. But after marriage, it is much harder to walk away. They may feel that their freedom is restricted.

Today, many couples accept the idea that living together before marriage is the best way to test the endurance of their commitment. They want a guarantee that everything will work out. But there are no guarantees in life or love, and often living together achieves the opposite of what is intended.

MYTH #3

Love conquers all—even a partner's greatest barriers to self-esteem.

Tina was a woman with low self-esteem. She had a history of failed relationships and she finally sought counseling to find out why she always seemed to choose men who belittled her. Her relationships normally followed a set pattern. The men treated her well in the beginning of the relationship, but as they got to know her, they treated her worse and worse. This only reinforced her deep-seated view that she was essentially worthless. It was a message that had been hammered home all her life—first by her parents, then by the teachers at school, and now by the men she met. She wanted the counselor to help her find a way she could present herself to men that would mask her many inadequacies.

The counselor recognized the pattern in the way men's attitudes toward Tina changed over time. And after several months of therapy, Tina began to see for herself that she was seriously misreading the course of her relationships. Because of her poor self-image, she was baiting men to treat her poorly. When men treated her well, she responded in a way that suggested she didn't think much of their judgment, either of herself or of people in general. When, in turn, they demeaned her, she reinforced their behavior, subconsciously indicating that their appraisal was on target. Because the men were rewarded for treating her poorly, their behavior became shaped by the reward system Tina set up. They treated her in the way she thought she deserved. But ironically, when they won her, they lost her. Once they treated her badly enough, she either left them, claiming she was being demeaned, or they left her, having bought the message that she wasn't good enough for them.

This self-destructive dance is not uncommon in relationships where one person has a problem with self-esteem. But it is contrary to the popular wisdom, which suggests that a person with a low opinion of himself or herself need only receive positive reinforcement to bolster his or her self-esteem. Why did Tina not respond to the positive feedback she received from men early in her relationships?

A person with low self-esteem is more likely to feel comfortable with a partner who reinforces his or her self-story than with someone who presents a challenge to that self-image. It is too threatening to be bombarded with new data that are affirming. Without being aware of it, persons with low self-esteem tend to choose partners who feel as they do. When they are paired with a person who thinks too highly of them, they find it impossible to cope with the clash in views. They cannot bring themselves to trust someone whose view of them is in such contrast to their own.

Tina automatically mistrusted men who built her up. She assumed they were only nice to her because they didn't know her well enough to see her many failings. Or, even worse, she suspected they might be deliberately deceiving her, leading her on in order to get something from her. Changing Tina's view of herself was a task that required several years of therapy. Her self-story was too deeply rooted. It was not enough, as our romantic mythology would have it, for a loving man to come along, sweep her off her feet, and shower her with affirmation.

It is a common relationship myth that one person can change the other by the sheer force of his or her love. But when one person is suffering from low self-esteem or other blocks to intimacy, a solution cannot be forced from the outside. We like to believe that we can rescue our loved ones and eliminate these barriers. We like to believe that love—specifically, *our* love—can conquer all. But true change and growth must come from within. It cannot be controlled from the outside, no matter how hard we try.

This myth is often acted out with couples when one person is addicted to alcohol or drugs. A woman whose husband was an alcoholic once told me, "I know he drinks because he doesn't have enough confidence in himself. If I can show him that I really love and respect him for who he is, he might not need to drink so much." This woman had been trying to do just that for five years, to no avail. Her words of support sounded hollow to her husband, and often he resented her for her attempts to control him. She, in turn, resented him for not getting better. Until she acknowledged that her husband's addiction was beyond her power to change, she would continue to be trapped in this destructive relationship.

MYTH #4

Religion is no longer as important to marital harmony
as it once was.

Data collected by myself and Sandi Wright, my research assistant at Yale, indicate that, contrary to popular belief, the importance of religion is not declining in
marriage. In one of our studies, we examined those
factors that either increase or decrease in importance
over the course of a relationship. Our premise was that
one of the reasons relationships decline over time is
that the partners are less matched in the factors that
matter later than they are in the factors that matter
earlier. We found that, of all the factors that increased
in importance over time, a match in religious beliefs
was the most important, outranking all the other variables.

Sam and Janet were deeply in love and they got
married in spite of the differences in their religious
backgrounds. Sam was Jewish and Janet was Roman
Catholic. They considered themselves a modern couple
who could handle the differences easily. But when their
first child was born, tension began to erupt in their
comfortable arrangement. They decided to raise the
child in both religious traditions, but this was easier
said than done. For the first time, they confronted the
fact that each would have to participate in and tolerate
the other's tradition. Matters came to a head when Sam
refused to stay in the house during Christmas if Janet
insisted on putting up a tree and a crèche. He had
never realized how upset he would become over seeing
his child participate in the Christian celebration.

In the beginning, the partners may be able to handle
their disagreement over religious beliefs, but they find

it more difficult when children enter the picture. At this point, each partner may want the children to be raised in his or her own faith, to be provided with some kind of solid spiritual ground. The problem is likely to be especially acute when major religious differences exist —such as marriage between a Christian and a Jew.

Of course, mixed-faith marriages that work do exist. But the myth that love is enough to cover even the greatest compromises is not always true. If compromises are made early in the marriage to please a partner, they may later become a source of dissatisfaction, especially if the partner's practices represent cultural and value systems that are not part of the person's background. We have become so comfortable in our secularized society that often we do not realize, until long into a relationship, how deep our roots really are.

This point can also be applied to relationships in which the partners have strong differences in important values. I have often heard people complain, "We don't seem to speak the same language." What they might really be saying is, "We don't believe in the same things." Couples who don't share a common fundamental "story" about life will find it hard to maintain their intimacy over time.

MYTH #5

One of the best ways to find out what kind of partner someone will make is to consider the household he or she was raised in.

Isn't it reasonable to suppose that being raised in a close and loving family will present an advantage in adult relationships? After all, a person who grew up with good family role models would be more likely to bring those qualities into a marriage.

But upbringing is only one of many variables that affects adult relationships. And what matters most is not the experiences you have had but what you have learned from those experiences.

I know a woman, Jane, who had a troubled childhood. Her father was an alcoholic who abused her both physically and verbally. Her mother could not face what was happening in her home and she feigned ignorance of the damage being inflicted upon her daughter.

As an adult, Jane chose to use her experiences in a positive way. With the help of therapy, she learned to see her background as an example of how not to behave in a relationship. She was determined not to repeat the mistakes of her parents. She's a loving and caring woman who has filled the vacuum of positive role models left by her parents with other adults.

In the same way that Jane turned a negative upbringing into a positive force, the reverse also happens. We can be disappointed when we depend on narrow criteria to judge whether or not someone will make a good partner.

Some people are obsessed with the past. Indeed, they might spend a lifetime in therapy only as an excuse to find ways of placing blame on others for their lack of success. ("My parents were not warm and loving, and that's why I can never be warm and loving.") But the past is, quite literally, *past*. Its only value to the present and the future is as a reference point. People are only victims of the past when they choose to be.

MYTH #6

Passion and sex are most important at the beginning
of a relationship.

Eric had dated a number of women before he started
going out with Stephanie, and he tended to choose so-
phisticated, experienced women. Stephanie was different from the other women, but Eric was charmed by
her shyness and lack of experience. He enjoyed the
role of being her teacher and she felt secure in the
hands of a man who could take charge and help her
overcome her awkwardness. Although their sexual relationship lacked the easy passion Eric was used to, it
seemed to fill both of their needs.

But over time, Eric began to feel frustrated because
Stephanie never became the kind of lover he had hoped
for. And Stephanie was equally frustrated. Although
Eric expressed passion in sex, she felt he lacked the
capacity for intimacy. The sexual relationship that had
worked earlier became a barrier later on.

The data I have collected indicate that the role of
passion and sex increases in importance during the
middle years of a marriage. Two to five years into the
relationship, passion and sex are even more important
than they were at the beginning.

Early on, in the first blush of romance, people tend
to overlook or make light of the flaws they perceive in
their partners. They believe that, over time, the rough
edges will be smoothed out. But as time goes on, the
flaws that once seemed unimportant become more and
more disturbing.

People tend to be especially critical and demanding
when it comes to sex. As the initial "wow" wears off,
they may feel restless and sex may seem routine. It is

then that passion takes on more importance. The fabled "seven-year itch" (which often occurs after four or five years) is in part due to the decline in passion. When Eric and Stephanie felt their relationship foundering, they sought the help of a sex therapist who taught them that passion and sex must grow and mature in a relationship or it will grow cold.

MYTH #7

"Chemistry" is the unpredictable wild card
in a relationship.

We usually think of chemistry as a mysterious "wild card"—totally unpredictable. But scientific research indicates that we tend to repeat the attachment styles we developed in infancy in our adult relationships. When we believe the myth that love "happens" to us, we fail to recognize—and avoid—destructive patterns.

Jeffrey Young, a brilliant psychotherapist in New York City, has devised a form of therapy called "schema therapy." According to Young, all of us grow up with "early maladaptive schemas," resulting from early experiences coping with life. One such schema, called vulnerability, leads a person to perceive constant threats to his or her personal integrity, whether they be financial, emotional, intellectual, occupational, or some other. Such a person may have grown up feeling insecure or seeing weaknesses or helplessness in those around him or her. Another schema, abandonment, is likely to result from feelings of being left alone and helpless in childhood. It is the fear that those who are most loved will leave and it leads to a reluctance to commit totally to love. Other schemas include dependence, fear of losing emotional control, unlovability, emotional deprivation, social exclusion, sexual undesirability, mistrust, poor judgment, incompetence, shame/inferiority, unrealistic standards, excessive self-control, guilt, inadequate self-discipline, and unrealistic freedom.

When people talk about "chemistry" in a relationship, they are often not aware that one predictable aspect of chemistry is the tendency to seek out and feel attraction for people who reinforce our early maladaptive schemas. These schemas, typically primitive and subconscious, cling to us like electrostatically charged underwear. They are so much a part of our identity that, even if we are aware of them, we are often reluctant to give them up—which, according to Young, is one of the reasons we are attracted to those people who reinforce them.

Not all early schemas are maladaptive. But chemistry has a way of generating explosive reactions—and those reactions often play upon early maladaptive schemas.

Lucy learned from the time she was very young that the best way to survive in her family was to avoid getting too close to anyone. The relationships in her family were cool—whenever a family member would start to get too close, other members would back off. It was believed that family members should treat one another with respect, which meant no meddling in personal matters. Lucy's parents were distant and discouraged open displays of affection; as Lucy grew up, she preferred to maintain some distance from other people. When she entered into romantic relationships, she found herself attracted to men who could not deal with being close. Although she admired men who could relate to her intimately, she found that they didn't turn her on. Thus, chemical reactions were following Lucy's early maladaptive schema of seeking distance, even when she consciously desired intimacy.

According to Mary Ainsworth, a professor at the University of Virginia who has studied infant-attachment patterns, an infant who is separated from his or her mother for relatively brief periods of time tends to react in one of three ways when the mother reenters the room. One type, the secure infant, seeks out the mother gladly, showing only minor distress at having been separated. The secure infant contrasts with the avoidant infant, who, upon the mother's return, actively avoids her. Both of these infants are in contrast to the anxious/ambivalent infant, who desperately seeks out the mother upon her return, and has tremendous difficulty in dealing with the separation.

What does this have to do with adult relationships? Phillip Shaver, Ph.D., of the State University of New York at Buffalo and his colleagues have found that we tend to repeat in our adulthood the attachment style we developed in infancy. The adult who was secure as an infant will tend to be secure as an adult. But the adult who was either avoidant or anxious/ambivalent in infancy will tend to recapitulate these schemas in adulthood. The chemistry of a relationship, therefore, is at least somewhat predictable.

Research by Elliot Blass and his colleagues at Johns Hopkins University takes the question of chemistry one step further. Although his research was done with rats, it is conceivable that the results of the research may extend to humans. Blass studied baby rats born to mothers who had been immersed in a certain odorant. When the baby rats grew up and sought mates, they preferred rats that had been immersed in the same odorant as their mothers. In other words, the smell associated with the mother seemed to influence the chemical bonding of a rat with a mate.

Although we have a long way to go in understanding the phenomenon of chemistry—what attracts one person to another—we are beginning to understand that many predictable elements are involved. Chemistry does not appear to be the "wild card" in relationships that we once believed it to be.

MYTH #8

The ability to communicate will improve as you get to know one another better.

As Harry and Ellen grew closer, Harry found himself opening up to Ellen about his past, including telling her about some of his bizarre sexual exploits. Harry had a voracious appetite for sex and had gotten himself into situations that made for interesting telling, especially when he found that Ellen was willing to accept him and his background.

Over time, Harry found himself less and less able to stay faithful to Ellen and he started regularly seeing other women on the side. Ellen wanted an exclusive relationship, but Harry, although he didn't want to lose Ellen, still longed for the adventures of the past.

Harry was able to be completely frank with Ellen about his past relationships, but he was like a clam when it came to leveling with her about his current activities. He was afraid of losing her and it was too big a risk to tell her what was happening. He became more and more secretive about his feelings and his activities. When Ellen eventually found out he was seeing other women, she left him, not so much because of what he was doing, but because he had broken faith with her by not telling the truth.

It often happens in relationships that the closer we become, the more we feel we have to lose by communicating honestly with one another. At the start of the relationship, we may hold back from disclosing our deepest, darkest secrets. As we get to know a person more intimately, we are more willing to tell him or her things about ourselves that perhaps we thought we would never reveal. But then, as time goes on, there is a tendency to close up again because we feel vulnerable to our loved one's opinion of us. If communication and trust are not established early in the relationship, we cannot hope that they will develop later when the stakes are much higher.

Many people harbor a secret view that, if people knew their "true self," they would not find it attractive. To a certain extent, we all wear public masks that allow us to present our most acceptable selves to the world. Choosing to trust another person enough to drop the masks is not easy, for we risk the possibility that our "true selves" will be rejected. But unless we are willing to drop our masks from the start, we can easily become mired in a web of deception. And even small deceptions become meaningful when they close doors on our ability to communicate.

I know a man who told his wife, "I will share everything about myself with you except my experiences during the war. They're too hard to talk about." He could not see that by closing that door, he was making true communication impossible. His wife never felt as though she really knew him.

I know another man who committed a relatively small deception, but one that had great impact on his life. When he first met the woman he eventually married, he lied about his age, subtracting eight years. During the thirty years they were married, he never admitted the truth and went to great pains to make sure his wife never found out his real age. He took his secret with him to the grave, and it was only when his wife saw the death certificate that she learned the truth. She told me, sadly, "I can understand why he didn't tell me in the beginning. I might have thought he was too old for me. But later, when we were happily married and very close, he should have been able to trust me with the truth. Could he have really thought it would have mattered to me then?"

MYTH #9

Spouses should love and like one another more than they love and like other people.

In a study conducted at Yale, Susan Grajek, a former graduate student, and I investigated the patterns of liking and loving among men and women for various people in their lives—including parents, romantic partners, siblings closest in age, and best friends of the same sex. We found different patterns for men and women.

Men showed the pattern that was most predictable. They both liked and loved their romantic partner the most. Best friends of the same sex came in second, followed by their father, then their mother. They liked and loved their siblings closest in age the least.

Women also liked and loved their sibling closest in age the least and slightly preferred their mother over their father. But the most surprising result was the finding that women loved their best friend of the same sex as much as they loved their romantic partner of the opposite sex. And they actually liked their best friend of the same sex more than they liked their romantic partner. Why might this be true?

It is well known that women seek more intimacy and are better at attaining it than men. For women, intimacy is important, not only in romantic relationships, but in close friendships as well. Men are more likely to seek intimacy in romantic relationships and are content to find their best friend in their romantic partner.

Why might some women like their best friend of the same sex more than their romantic partner? If a woman is involved with a man who cannot communicate with her at the level of intimacy she seeks, she may find herself able to be closer on certain levels with a woman friend.

Nan and Adam both value open communication in their relationship. But they have different ideas about what constitutes good communication. Nan likes to express her feelings and say what she feels about various people in her life, including Adam. What she has to say is not always positive, but she believes that a good relationship is one in which people express their feelings toward each other, both good and bad.

Adam feels threatened when Nan expresses dissatisfaction with their relationship. He believes that communicating negative feelings only undermines a good relationship. He views good communication as expressing support and sharing the events of the day.

Both Nan and Adam value good communication, but they have different ideas about what that means. This results in conflict. Nan accuses Adam of dealing only with the superficial aspects of life. Adam feels that Nan is undermining their relationship by shooting holes in it. Nan is dissatisfied with Adam's conception of intimacy, and Adam is dissatisfied with Nan's dissatisfaction with him.

Nan seeks the intimacy she lacks in her marriage from her close friends, and she depends upon them to provide the feedback she doesn't get from Adam. This pattern is common in relationships, and sometimes it is quite healthy. But if outside friends become a substitute for intimacy that should be present in a marriage, the couple must examine why. Nan's justification for depending on her friends for intimacy is not unlike the justification of a man who has an affair and says, "I love my wife, but my sexual needs are greater than she can fill."

On the other hand, a healthy couple will embrace the larger community of friends, family, and co-workers and acknowledge that no one person is capable of filling all of their needs. We seek out different people for different reasons, and sometimes the presence of a close friend can serve as a valuable balancing point that actually strengthens a primary relationship. When we believe that our romantic partner should always be the person we like and love most, and who likes and loves us most, we are implying that there is an element of "ownership" in relationships—that our partner belongs to us emotionally. This leads to a deterioration of the relationship as it becomes characterized by jealousy and fear.

MYTH #10

The best way to judge how your partner feels about you is to observe his or her actions.

Larry shopped for an engagement ring for Julia. He looked at a variety of diamond rings, but found them uninteresting. He couldn't understand how a stone that just looked like a fancy piece of glass could sell for so much money. He wanted a stone that showed how he really felt, that was unique and special. One day he came upon an antique turquoise ring that was an estate piece dating back about 200 years. It was marvelously hand-crafted, and its intricate design showed a degree of care he felt could not be found in any of the contemporary rings he had looked at. He happily bought the ring, planning to surprise Julia with his originality.

He succeeded on the first score. Julia was certainly surprised. But her reaction was nothing like what he had anticipated. She appreciated Larry's good intentions, but she could not hide her deep disappointment. She didn't see the symbolism in Larry's gesture. For her engagement, she wanted a diamond—that was an important symbol to her. In spite of her disappointment, Julia accepted the ring and they were married.

Three years later, Larry gave Julia a diamond eternity ring which she started wearing as a wedding band. Larry and Julia are still happily married. They find they share many things in common, although taste in jewelry isn't one of them.

The point of this story is to illustrate that the very same action can symbolize different things to different people. For example, holding hands in public may be interpreted as a sign of affection on the part of one partner, but as a showy and inappropriate display by the other. Or one partner might view daily lovemaking as a sign of deeper love, while the other sees it as a dull routine. Often in relationships, an action means completely different things to the two partners. As such, the saying that "actions speak louder than words" is not necessarily accurate. It is not always possible to interpret a person's feelings by the way he or she acts.

Our acceptance of the false myths about love often gets in the way of our having effective relationships.

- When we believe our feelings are enough, we miss the vital signals that tell us what we really expect and need in a relationship.

- When we decide that living together before marriage will guarantee a smooth relationship, we sometimes fail to internalize our commitment to one another.

- When we think we can force our partner to change, we do not see that change must come from within.

- When we think our love for one another is separate from our beliefs and values, we might be confronted with our pasts later in the relationship.

- When we make assumptions about a partner's suitability based on our observations about his or her family background, we are using limited and inaccurate criteria.

- When we believe that passion and sex are most important at the beginning of a relationship, we sometimes allow inertia to set in as time goes on.

- When we allow ourselves to feel helpless against the flow of chemistry, we fail to acknowledge the negative triggers over which we have control.

- When we assume that good communication and trust will develop over time, we ignore the danger signals that might be present early in the relationship.

- When we depend on our partner to fill all our needs, we exclude other people who can be important in our lives.

- When we assume that actions are the sole indicator of feelings, we easily draw false conclusions from the way people behave.

The point of this exercise in myth-shattering is to show what happens when we don't have Relationship Intelligence. We become swept away by common myths, easily swayed by the force of popular belief. It becomes harder and harder to recognize for ourselves what is real in matters of the heart.

Take a few moments to consider whether or not you have been allowing the false myths about relationships to rule your love life:

——————— QUIZ ———————

Are You Bound by Love Myths?

Consider the situations below and put a circle around the letter that best represents your attitude.

1. You know that your love is real when
   (a) you want to spend every minute possible with your loved one.
   (b) you share a close bond that you are committed to develop over a long period.
   (c) when you say "I love you," you really mean it.
   (d) you and your loved one share a deep attraction that is almost electric.

2. The best way to test the strength of your commitment is
   (a) to give up other activities so you can spend more time together.
   (b) your willingness to make compromises for the sake of your partner.
   (c) to live together and find out how well you interact on a day-to-day basis.

(d) to trust your partner with your most closely guarded secrets.

3. Your partner just got fired and is feeling a loss of self-esteem. You
   - (a) try to boost your partner's morale by putting down his or her employer.
   - (b) suggest that maybe he or she should look for less challenging work.
   - (c) offer support, but realize that your partner has to work things out on his or her own.
   - (d) call several business acquaintances and tell them your partner needs a job.

4. Having a shared belief system or religious background is
   - (a) very important in a relationship.
   - (b) somewhat important in a relationship.
   - (c) not very important in a relationship.
   - (d) not important at all in a relationship.

5. Your partner grew up in a warm, loving family. This tells you
   - (a) he or she is very likely to make a good partner.
   - (b) nothing measurable about his or her potential as a partner.
   - (c) he or she might be better equipped for partnership than someone who was raised in an unstable family.
   - (d) he or she is a warm, loving person.

6. During a long-term relationship, sexual passion
   - (a) is most important in the beginning, but is expected to diminish with time.
   - (b) should be strong in the beginning, and remain strong throughout the relationship.
   - (c) will be strong in the beginning, or not at all.
   - (d) is more important later in the relationship than it is in the beginning.

7. Your attraction to another person is
   - (a) partially the result of predictable patterns in your behavior and preferences.
   - (b) a mysterious happening that you can't explain.
   - (c) the result of a physical and emotional "chemistry."
   - (d) never something you can predict.

8. Open, honest communication
    (a) is easiest after you have been with someone for a long time.
    (b) is a great risk at the beginning of a relationship.
    (c) is best established when you begin to feel comfortable with another person.
    (d) is impossible until you feel absolutely secure in your relationship.

9. Your romantic partner should be
    (a) the most important friend you have.
    (b) a person who likes to do the same things you do.
    (c) on exactly the same wavelength as you are.
    (d) a person you care for in a special way that is distinct from others in your life.

10. Your partner's actions
    (a) are the best evidence of his or her love.
    (b) are not as reliable an indicator as his or her intentions.
    (c) are the window to his or her true feelings.
    (d) always speak louder than words.

Scoring:

Give yourself 1 point for each of the following statements that you circled:

1. b	5. b	8. c
2. b	6. d	9. d
3. c	7. a	10. b
4. a		

If you scored between 8 and 10 points, you are probably not a person who tends to be susceptible to common myths about love. If you scored between 4 and 7 points, you are somewhat susceptible. Chances are, you often feel confused about what to believe and what not to believe when it comes to love. If you scored less than 4, you have bought many of the common love myths.

But even if your score is low, you shouldn't feel that you are ill-equipped to master Relationship Intelligence. Actually, it is no surprise that people so readily cling to myths about love. There is a vast hole in our education when it comes to interpersonal relationships.

CHAPTER TWO

HEART SMART

THE INTELLIGENCE YOU NEVER LEARNED IN SCHOOL

Jim's wife is going to divorce him. He just learned this and he's mad as hell. He's also depressed and, most of all, perplexed. Why is this happening? From his perspective, the marriage is everything it should be. He and Maureen have two beautiful children, two good incomes, a lovely house, a solid position in their community, leisure time to relax and enjoy life, and lots of friends. Nevertheless, Maureen has told Jim she is not happy and wants to leave him. In spite of several long and arduous conversations, each lasting deep into the night, Jim still can't comprehend why Maureen is dissatisfied. She says that if Jim can't see what's wrong, he's just plain dumb.

Is Jim dumb? Certainly not by any measurable standards. He graduated cum laude from his university and is a successful lawyer employed by a major corporate firm. He was a star in college and he is a star in his career. He certainly doesn't fit the profile of someone who is "just plain dumb."

But look at things from Maureen's point of view. During the last five years of their eight-year marriage, Maureen has been expressing dissatisfaction. For example, she has told Jim repeatedly that she wants to spend more relaxed time with him, whether at home or on vacation. But when they take vacations, Jim always manages to stay glued to the phone, making deals for his clients and for himself. Maureen has also pleaded with him to help more with raising their children. He has agreed, but his reformed behavior never lasts for more than a few days. Maureen has tried to talk to Jim about her concerns regarding their relationship. Sometimes Jim hears, but she feels he never really listens.

Maureen believes there is a breakdown in communication. Jim believes they communicate quite well. He thinks Maureen complains too much, but he accepts it as part of her personality. Unfortunately, his acceptance no longer matters because the marriage is about to end. From Maureen's point of view, it really ended five years ago.

Jim is insulted when Maureen says he's dumb. "I graduated from law school. I passed the bar exam. How dumb could I be?" he argues. But the lack of smarts that Maureen observes in her husband has nothing to do with the kind of academic intelligence measured by traditional tests. Jim's deficiency is in Relationship Intelligence.

It's no wonder that we don't know how to use our intelligence in love—we never learned how. Love skills are not taught in school. It is assumed that we will learn all we need to know from observation, or that the skills will come automatically. But observation is only one small part of learning. There is no place where we learn how to evaluate our observations; they remain subjective, often reinforcing our notions that love is "supposed to be" a certain way.

In short, being "school smart" does not mean we'll be "love smart." Let's examine the traditional learning methods and see why they don't necessarily work when we try to apply them to our relationships.

We don't learn problem recognition

The teacher poses a problem; the student solves it.

The textbook poses questions at the end of each chapter; the student answers them.

The test consists of 100 recall questions; the student remembers the facts and answers them.

In a typical classroom, the student is never required to recognize the problem. The problem is already presented by the teacher or on the test or in the textbook. The task of the student is to solve it after it is identified.

Life is different. We must be able to recognize problems and if we can't, we're going to run into trouble. In the illustration above, we see that Jim had this difficulty. Maureen had given him plenty of signals that things were not right with their marriage, but he simply did not recognize the problem.

Consider another example. Alex walked out of his marriage to Leona three years ago when he fell in love with another woman. He told Leona he wanted a divorce so he could marry his lover. But Alex's relationship with the other woman ended soon after he and Leona were divorced. Then, suddenly, he began to behave in a very sweet and attentive way toward Leona, and she took his behavior to mean that perhaps a reconciliation was imminent. But after three years, it still had not happened. Leona was still hoping. Alex continued to indicate that there was still a chance of their getting back together. But he made it clear that he was not yet ready to be pinned down. He continued to date other women. Meanwhile, Leona was directing all her attention toward a reconciliation and had put her own social life on hold.

According to Leona, "I have no problem with Alex. He's the one with a problem. He fell out of love with me; I never fell out of love with him." Leona was unable to recognize that, indeed, she did have a problem. She had put her life on hold for an eventuality that would probably never occur. The longer Leona continued to insist that there was no problem, the more deeply set in her false conviction she became.

Problem recognition is far more complex than it might seem at first glance. You might observe a situation and ask, "Isn't it obvious that something is wrong?" But it's not always so obvious. Consider the dilemma faced by a person whose spouse is an alcoholic. The alcoholic's partner might repeatedly point out the problem, might beg and plead, might say, "Can't you see that your drinking is ruining our marriage?" But the wisdom of those who counsel alcoholics is clear: The alcoholic must admit (that is, *recognize*) that there is a problem before there is any hope of treatment.

We don't learn how to define the scope of the problem

Once it is recognized that something is wrong, the task is to define the scope of the problem. Problem definition involves deciding which aspects of the problem require attention. Again, most textbook problems are defined clearly; we understand from the outset the arenas in which they occur. In fact, in many of the practical domains of life, we define problems somewhat automatically. For example, if you have a problem receiving certain television programs, you (or the technician you hire) can define the problem quite accurately as the need for a new antenna or better placement of the antenna, or the need to replace your set, or maybe the need for cable television.

How you define a problem often depends on the amount of information and the resources you have available to you, as well as the number of possibilities you are willing to consider. Your definition of the problem is intricately linked to the course you set for its solution. That is why, once you've defined a problem, it is often hard to change your course of action.

If problem definition seems to be a matter of common sense in day-to-day life, it gets murkier in the arena of relationships. Say, for example, that you've done something that you know will incite anger or disapproval on the part of your partner. How do you define the problem? It is tempting to define it as the need to conceal your action to prevent the likely repercussions. But this definition will almost surely lead to more problems.

Lorraine found herself in this situation in the aftermath of a brief affair. It had been "one of those things," and she had cut it off quickly because she really believed in monogamy and she loved her husband. She defined the problem as the possibility that her husband would find out about the affair, be deeply hurt, and maybe even leave her. She decided not to tell him about it and just let the affair fade into obscurity. But she didn't count on the strong feelings of her lover, who was determined to win her back and began calling her at the office and then at home. Lorraine's husband was puzzled by the strange phone calls and her flustered behavior. And one day, when Lorraine inadvertently wore a pin her lover had given her, he commented that he had never known her to buy jewelry for herself. She broke down and told him the truth. As she had suspected, he was deeply hurt. But what surprised her was that he was not as hurt about the brief and meaningless affair as he was about Lorraine's dishonesty. "If you had told me, I would have tried to understand," he said. Lorraine realized that she had misdefined the problem by focusing on keeping the affair a secret.

We learn to view problems as well-structured

When I was a teenager, I saw an advertisement in a newspaper that promised handwriting analysis for just $10.95. I decided to send in a sample of my handwriting. I got the analysis back a few weeks later. For the most part, it told me what I or anyone else would want to hear about him or herself. It pointed out lots of glorious strengths (which it noted other people did not always recognize) together with a few weaknesses, all minor, of course!

I wondered how the company that did the handwriting analysis could make any money by selling this service for just $10.95. I soon found out. Enclosed with the analysis was a letter noting that I had many positive attributes and a few negative ones. Undoubtedly, the letter said, I would want to take advantage of the opportunity to make my personality even better than it was. Indeed, I could rid myself of my few undesirable traits simply by changing my handwriting! If I signed up for the handwriting lessons the company was offering, soon my handwriting would correspond to a more positive personality structure, and I would have this better personality.

The story is amusing in retrospect, but I tell it to illustrate how often in life we are tempted by ways to turn "ill-structured" problems into "well-structured" problems. The idea that the messy dilemmas of our lives can be simply solved by changing our handwriting or our hair color or by any number of other easy methods is quite appealing.

It is a constant source of frustration that the problems of life tend to be so ill-structured. We tend to resent the fact that they are not like those problems we solved in the classroom. In school, we dealt with well-structured problems—that is, there were clear steps guaranteed to lead to a solution. But in life, there is usually no clear path to a single solution. Often, it is not even clear whether there is a solution at all.

The people who gain the most from our believing that there is a single well-structured path to the solution of real-life problems are those who are out to sell a product or concept. They promote "ten easy steps to . . ." or lure us into purchasing a product that will help us lose weight, stop smoking, or whatever we are looking for to change our lives. We buy the products and read the books because we want so much to believe that a prescribed solution does exist. But the single-solution road never leads to permanent satisfaction.

Take a common ill-structured life problem—how to fight boredom in your sex life. You've been to bed with your partner many times and the pizzazz is wearing off. It's not as thrilling the hundredth time as it was the first. This is not a well-defined problem, since there are no ten easy steps to a solution that are guaranteed to work for everyone. Certainly, there are things you can do to bring excitement back into your sex life. But what works for you won't necessarily work for someone else —or even work again for you at a different time in your life.

Susan knew that Ben was bored with her in bed. She thought it might be due to the extra weight she'd gained since the birth of their children. She felt fat and unattractive and she suspected he found her that way, too. Determined to change things in the bedroom, she went on a rigorous diet and exercise program, and after a few months she had lost weight and was looking and feeling better than ever. Ben flattered her on her new look, but to Susan's dismay, her improved appearance didn't renew Ben's passion in bed. Susan was angry, bitter, and confused. She had thrown herself into the task of improving her body to put a new spark of passion into their marriage, and her efforts had not changed anything.

Susan fell into the trap of believing that a better body automatically leads to a more passionate sex life—a conception that is reinforced daily by the popular media. But passion is not automatically triggered by physical appearance. Ben and Susan's problems in the bedroom were complex. They could not be solved by a single superficial change.

We don't learn to examine the context of a problem

Conventional intelligence tests sometimes include "transitive–inference" problems. For example, you're told that Crispy Flakes cereal is better than Crunchy Flakes cereal, but Soggy Flakes cereal is not as good as Crunchy Flakes—then you're asked which is the best or the worst. These problems require that you make an inference from the data presented and assume that no other data are needed to reach an accurate conclusion. These are direct problems of logic that do not involve extenuating circumstances or value judgments.

Real-world problems are not like this. They exist within a complex network of circumstances. For example, if you are in the process of buying a house, you cannot express everything you need to know in a couple of sentences. You need to examine many things—house prices, interest rates, property values, schools, proximity to services, home style preferences, and so on. Real-world problems differ from textbook problems in the amount of context you need to solve them. If you ignore this and assume that there is an ideal that exists apart from the contextual issues, you run into problems. This happens frequently when you try to simplify your problems with logic that is drawn from false premises. People often do this when they are looking for a mate, saying, for example, that a certain type of person will make a better lover or partner. We've all heard people say things like, "I only date men who are tall," or "I'm looking for a slender, blond woman." The personal ads in newspapers are filled with such statements. But when you begin with a false premise, you're likely to be disappointed when your expectations are not met. Furthermore, you automatically close off the possibilities that might otherwise be available to you.

The context in which a relationship occurs rubs off on the relationship. If the context is a favorable one, it tends to help the relationship; if it is unfavorable, it tends to hurt the relationship.

A recent event in my own life illustrates how the surrounding context of a situation can influence a person's feelings about a relationship. I had gone to another city on business and was supposed to be met at the airport by a woman who would be my hostess for the couple of days I would be there. Because of mixed signals, she was not there to meet me and I ended up waiting outside the airport for an hour. After we finally connected, she drove me to my hotel, which was nothing great. But that was more than you could say for the people who populated the hotel lobby. To put it mildly, their primary purpose for being there did not appear to be to get a good night's sleep—or even to stay for the entire night. My hostess then took me to dinner. After finding several restaurants closed or too crowded, we finally found a place where the food was lousy. By the time I left the city, I had less than the warmest feelings for my hostess. She really hadn't done anything wrong. But the environment had spoiled the relationship I had with her. No matter how hard she might have tried to be personally pleasing, the context of the setting had rubbed off on our relationship.

We learn to depend on "right" and "wrong" answers

Academic problems often come equipped with right and wrong answers. Indeed, on standardized tests, it would be unsuitable not to have a single correct answer. If you score well on tests by getting many or all of the answers right, you are rewarded. This conditioning leads many people to value the idea of finding right answers to their problems. But in everyday life, problems rarely have one right solution. Usually, there are a number of possible ways to address a problem and it is difficult—except in hindsight—to know which one is best.

In academic testing situations, the answers you pick determine the outcome. But in real life, it's often how you follow through on the solution that matters. Even decisions that in hindsight seem to have been less than prescient can be made more effective by a different or more creative use of the resources provided. By the same token, decisions that appear excellent can be undermined by a poor use of resources.

Frank and Joanne have reached an impasse in an ongoing argument about where they should live. Joanne is pregnant with their first child, and she believes that they should move out of their city apartment and purchase a home in a smaller community. "The city is not a good place to raise children," she says, with absolute conviction. Frank disagrees. He grew up in the city, and he tells Joanne, "The city is the best place to raise children."

Both Frank and Joanne are certain they are right, but this is an issue that doesn't have a right or wrong answer. Even if one of them argued that, statistically, one or the other location was better for certain aspects of child raising, there could never be any real proof. Ultimately, a wide variety of factors will come into play to determine whether Frank and Joanne are "successful" parents.

In a deeply personal decision, such as whether or not to have children, where to live, and what career to pursue, there is no single right answer. What matters most is the way you follow through on the decision, not the decision itself. Many people who avoid making a commitment to a partner because they are not "100 percent sure" it will work, might wait forever for such a guarantee.

We expect all information to be readily available

In school, and especially on tests, you are supposed to know the information you need to solve a problem, or at least have the information readily available. But in everyday life, it's not always clear where you can find the data you need. For example, if you are looking for a doctor, how do you find the information that will tell you whether a given individual is a good doctor? You could try to find out where the doctor received his or her medical degree. But a degree, even from a prestigious medical school, won't guarantee that the doctor will be good for you.

The same thing applies to personal relationships. How do you know whether someone will make a good partner? You can examine his or her past relationships, but that won't necessarily give you the information you need, since what is right for one person is not necessarily right for another. And what is right for you at one point in your life may be wrong for you later. What criteria do you use? Since it's often unclear how to find out the information you need to judge a relationship, the tendency is to rely heavily on "gut" instinct or emotions.

Early in a relationship, when you are still feeling freshly enamored of the other person, you might limit your ideas of what is relevant and make a judgment on a relatively superficial basis. This happened to Lisa and Phil, who were deeply in love. Their time together was very romantic, and they felt that they had all the information that was really important; what they didn't know, the starry-eyed couple assumed, they would discover later. Once they were married, Lisa and Phil *did* find out a lot more about each other. The information had been available all along, but they hadn't been looking for it. What they learned was that they had very little in common and had very different ideas about the roles of husband and wife. The more they learned about each other, the less starry-eyed they became. In the clear light of day-to-day living, Lisa and Phil could see that they were not a good match.

What information will tell us whether or not a person will make a good partner? Since we are unsure where to look, we often depend on immediate and superficial clues, or we use criteria that do not really cover all the important domains of life. Unlike the academic world, where the criteria are more objective, our personal lives are filled with subjective criteria that are hard to fit into reality.

We are discouraged from seeking input from others

In school, we are expected to solve problems on our own. In fact, solving problems any other way might be considered cheating. At least one standardized testing agency has uniformed security guards who go after people who seem to have collaborated with others during test-taking. As a result, we learn how to be good individual test-takers, but we don't necessarily become skillful at solving problems in collaboration with others.

Almost all real-world problem solving involves more than one person, and yet, as an outgrowth of our school days, many of us believe that it is better to try to solve problems alone.

In the university setting where I work, a premium is placed on the ability of individuals to solve problems independently. Hiring practices favor people who have shown they can do well when left on their own. But these people are often poorly equipped to work with others when it is required. Indeed, if a faculty member works closely with too many others in doing research, it might jeopardize his or her promotion. Others will begin to question which ideas are that person's and which belong to others. The concept of "ownership" of an idea works against the collaborative approach, and in this way the system works against the development of problem-solving skills that are relevant to relationships.

In work that Wendy Williams and I have done on "group intelligence," we have found that groups often do better than individuals when asked to devise a creative solution to a problem. We have also found that, when one member of the group is an "eager beaver"— that is, a strongly controlling, dominant participant— the group is less effective than when all members participate equally. Our research suggests that, in solving interpersonal problems, an independent or controlling thinker will not necessarily expedite a problem's resolution.

Paul is a psychotherapist, and he believes this gives him an edge in solving problems that come up in his marriage to Liz. When they argue, he often refers to his special expertise. He is confident that he knows how the problem should be handled, and usually he tries to control the resolution of every issue. Paul learned how to help people resolve their problems, but he never learned how to participate, in a collaborative way, in the problem-solving process. When Paul takes charge of the discussion, Liz feels resentful. She wishes that he would stop being an expert and start listening to her as a husband. Liz knows she will never feel content unless they work on solving their problems together.

We learn to value verbal over nonverbal communication

Schools emphasize the importance of verbal communication in the development of cognitive skills. When they don't have well-developed verbal skills, students are usually judged to be less intelligent. Clearly, verbal skills are important in life, but at the same time, we often ignore the importance of nonverbal skills.

Nonverbal signaling is a crucial part of relationships. Consider, for example, what occurs when there is trouble in a relationship. Almost without fail, the first signs that something is wrong are nonverbal. A partner might feel an emotion that he or she can't yet identify or doesn't know how to express verbally. But the subconscious recognition that something is wrong will most likely express itself nonverbally. Being sensitive to nonverbal signals can mean the difference between success and failure in a relationship.

Alice was afraid to tell Penn how frustrated she was with his moody behavior and his sharp temper. She could never find the words that would allow him to understand her point of view without him blowing up. Penn was satisfied that Alice had "finally stopped complaining all the time." But if he were sensitive to nonverbal communication, he would recognize by Alice's behavior and facial expressions that there was something wrong. Far from being a sign that their problems were settled, Alice's lack of verbal expression indicated that an even deeper problem existed between them.

We learn formal knowledge to the exclusion of informal knowledge

Schools emphasize formal knowledge—what is explicitly taught in the classroom, in textbooks, and through various fixed channels of instruction. Achievement tests measure almost exclusively the factual knowledge learned from the classroom. Isn't it ironic, then, that in everyday life, the standard knowledge of the classroom matters so little? Many people will agree that it is the informal knowledge picked up in life, not the formal knowledge learned in the classroom, that counts the most.

Interpersonal relationships are almost entirely dependent on informal knowledge. How do you learn what your partner enjoys and values? How do you learn the kinds of things that drive your partner crazy? How do you learn what works and doesn't work in your relationship? There is no body of formal knowledge that will give you the answers. You learn by being with your partner, observing, listening, getting to know him or her. Thus, the kind of knowledge you need to make a relationship work is exactly the kind you do not learn in school—informal knowledge.

The formal knowledge we learn in school is accompanied by a system of formal or deductive logic. But the informal logic that we use in relationships is not so cut and dried. Although we may reach conclusions based on premises we believe to be correct, the premises may be faulty or the conclusion based on incorrect logic.

In the formal logic of the classroom, we are given a premise which sets the stage for reaching a conclusion:

All men are mortal.
Socrates is a man.
Therefore, Socrates is mortal.

The premise that all men are mortal is acknowledged to be true, and the conclusion follows logically. But when we try to use this method of formal logic to evaluate relationships, one of two breakdowns tends to occur. Either we begin with a premise that is faulty, or we draw an illogical conclusion from an accurate premise.

The following is an example of a faulty premise that leads to a faulty conclusion:

All men cheat on their wives.
Jack is a man.
Therefore, Jack cheats on his wife.

Even when the premise is accurate, we don't always draw the logical conclusion:

Some men cheat on their wives.
Jack is a man.
Therefore, Jack cheats on his wife.

In the second example, the only conclusion that can be reached is that Jack *might* cheat on his wife. But even that may not be logical, given the body of informal knowledge that exists about Jack. Everything else that is known about Jack's personality, standards, and typical behavior might lead to the conclusion that it would be unlikely for Jack to cheat on his wife. No valid conclusion can be reached without applying informal logic.

Sharon used a faulty premise when she evaluated her husband, Paul's, recent lack of sexual interest. "He hasn't made love to me for two weeks, and when I try to get him interested, he says he's too tired," she complained. "We used to make love several times a week. I worry that he doesn't love me as much as he once did."

What was Sharon's logic?

Loving couples always make love several
times a week.
Sharon and Paul did not make love for two
weeks.
Therefore, Sharon and Paul are not a loving
couple.

But formal logic could not be applied to this circumstance, and when Sharon tried, her logic was bound to be faulty. Informal knowledge (or common sense) would tell her that there could be many reasons for Paul's current lack of interest in sex.

If someone tries to tell you that something about relationships must be true, given the rules of logic, you have good reason to be skeptical. In fact, formal, deductive logic is rarely useful in relationships. Informal logic is the backbone of almost all the conclusions you draw. You use it every day, usually many times. It is so much a part of you that you are probably not even aware that you are using it.

If, for example, your partner is usually grumpy before having morning coffee, you anticipate, on a daily basis, that he or she is probably going to be grumpy before having coffee in the morning. If your partner has a certain facial expression that he or she has always made to signal feelings of guilt, when you see that expression, you conclude that your partner probably feels guilty.

Informal logic, then, applies when there is no deductive certainty. We use it to draw conclusions that are true much of the time, but not necessarily all of the time.

We learn to view problems as neatly classified and easily solvable

Academic problems tend to be neatly classified and easy to isolate and solve. By contrast, real-life problems are messy, persistent, and complex. In school, you do the assignment, learn the material, and pass the test. That completes your concern with the problem and you go on to the next one. But in life, problems are seldom easily classified, isolated, or short-lived. How do you deal with a competitor who is edging in on your business or with a family member who interferes with your life or with a child who gets into trouble? These are messy problems and they are connected to other arenas of your life. For example, if you deal with your unhappiness at work by quitting your job, that solution has vast implications for your family and life-style. Solving one problem can lead to the creation of others.

Relationship problems can be particularly "messy," since there are few objective guidelines that help us to solve them. And problems are rarely isolated. Sheila and Barry decided that having a child would strengthen their marriage, which had been losing its luster. They prepared excitedly for the baby's birth, and indeed, when their son was born, they felt closer to one another than they had in a long time. But as time went on, it became clear that the presence of a child presented a whole new series of problems: They had less time together; money was tighter; they often disagreed about the proper ways to care for the baby. Their assumption that having a child would improve their marriage was a simplistic and ultimately unfeasible one. The complexity of life is such that problems cannot be singled out and destroyed like isolated enemies.

Now you can see why the academic preparation we get in school leaves us so poorly prepared for everyday life —especially when it comes to relationships. A comparison of Academic Intelligence with Relationship Intelligence shows that they differ in virtually every aspect:

ACADEMIC INTELLIGENCE	RELATIONSHIP INTELLIGENCE
1. Problems are predefined.	1. Problems must be recognized on their own, and their nature must be defined.

(Cont.)

ACADEMIC INTELLIGENCE	RELATIONSHIP INTELLIGENCE
2. Problems are usually presented in simple, well-structured ways.	2. Problems almost always have a degree of ambiguity. They are rarely presented in straightforward ways.
3. The context of problems is not necessarily a factor in determining their successful solution.	3. Relationship problems always exist within a broader context that influences both the way the problems are defined and the options available for their solutions.
4. Academic problems, especially those that appear on tests, are often judged to have specific "right" answers. These are not answers that we determine; rather, they are presented to us by others.	4. Relationship problems never have objectively "right" or "wrong" answers. They are solved by making choices from options. The choices themselves are not necessarily as important as the independent actions that follow.
5. Problems can be solved without necessarily knowing important details that exist in the background. For example, solving a mathematical formula requires knowledge of a method but not knowledge of abstract principles.	5. Background issues may dramatically affect one's understanding of a problem and the choice of solutions. Sometimes these background issues do not even exist in the same arena as the problem at hand.

(Cont.)

ACADEMIC INTELLIGENCE	RELATIONSHIP INTELLIGENCE
6. The ability to reach solutions independently is valued above reaching solutions in collaboration with others.	6. Solutions to relationship problems, by their very nature, require collaboration with another person or persons.
7. Data are presented in a rational way; they are articulated clearly and often verbally.	7. Data may be presented in a variety of ways, both clear and hazy. Nonverbal signals may have greater value than what is articulated verbally.
8. Academic learning is formal; that is, there are prescribed ranges of problems and set formulas and methods used for their solution.	8. In relationships, informal learning—the way humans learn to understand, listen to, and empathize with one another—is often more useful.
9. Problems have clear resolutions.	9. Problems are often messy and persistent; they may require ongoing resolutions, and the solution to one problem may create a new problem.

The principles and techniques that work so well in school may be the opposite of what is required to solve our real-life problems. It is no surprise, therefore, to find that the people who are most successful in school often have the most trouble outside it. And it answers the complaint many people have: "Why, if I'm so smart, am I so dumb in my relationships?"

Are "smart" people better at loving?

Clearly, academic skills are not the only determinant of intelligence, although they are the gauge we most commonly use. In my book, *The Triarchic Mind,* I define intelligence as a three-part dynamic. In addition to the ability to use logic and reason, the nature of intelligence includes two other components. These are the ability to apply common sense, or practical intelligence, and the ability to think creatively, using insight.

In the book, I present a number of exercises to enable readers to test their intelligence. A person who scores well in one or more of the three aspects of reason, practical application, and creativity might be considered "intelligent." It is reasonable to assume that the intelligent person will, on the whole, do better in life than the person who scores poorly in all components. Some degree of balance is best. Someone who is skilled in reasoning, but who lacks creativity, may be considered rigid; a highly creative person who lacks common sense may be considered "flaky." By nature, human intelligence is the balanced operation of this three-part dynamic.

An intelligent person may indeed have the edge on a less intelligent person, but by itself, intelligence does not guarantee relationship success. Relationship Intelligence includes other dynamics that are not necessarily included in the intelligence dynamic: empathy, passion, intimacy, the will to act, commitment, and intuition, among others. Relationship Intelligence also requires a certain context that might differ substantially from the one you use in other arenas of your life. For example, "common sense" on the job is often quite different from "common sense" in an interpersonal relationship.

The techniques of Relationship Intelligence, which are described later in this book, are uniquely suited to the real-life problems of love and relationships. They must be learned, just the way academic skills must be learned. You don't pick them up automatically. And, in the same way that school does not prepare you for love, your experience at work can also sabotage your ability to be effective in your relationships.

CHAPTER THREE

LOVE SAVVY

A STAR IN BUSINESS, A FAILURE IN LOVE

Frank was a veritable whiz kid at work; during his first year in sales he had nearly doubled his company's gross income. He was a talented salesman because he had an instinct for feeling out the customer, finding the need, and addressing it directly. Clients had told his boss that Frank's presentations were irresistible. But when it came to his relationships, Frank felt like a failure. Women were attracted to him, but the relationships never lasted beyond the initial courtship stage. Frank couldn't understand it. How could he be such a savvy businessman and such an ineffective lover?

The behavior and strategies we learn in the business world do not prepare us for success in relationships any more than do those we learn in school. This is seen clearly when we examine the work ideology.

We know when we're getting ahead

It is easy for Frank to know how he's doing on the job. The sales reports are published every month and his progress is all there in black and white. Most work situations include reasonably clear signposts that mark the road to progress. You can tell whether you are moving forward, standing still, or moving backward.

In relationships, it is usually hard to know when you are moving forward or backward. It is more like a maze where you have no clear idea in which direction you are going. In fact, sometimes when you think you've progressed, you find that you have really been moving backward. We are all so programmed to think in terms of success as an ascending line on a growth chart that we become frustrated with the circuitous path of relationships.

Frank feels confident on the job, but he misses the point when he tries to measure his marital success in the same way.

According to Frank, things are really moving forward for him and Susan. In the three years they've been married, they have both received promotions at work and their income has doubled. They have moved into a large house with a swimming pool and they have purchased a new car. Frank is ready to take the next step forward—having children—because now he feels that he and Susan are stable and in a position to provide well for them. But every time he brings up the subject of children, Susan makes excuses for why this isn't a good time. They argue about it frequently, and Frank can't understand his wife's reluctance.

When Susan suggests they see a marriage counselor, Frank is shocked. For him, their lives have never been better. But what he perceives as "moving forward" has looked a lot different to Susan. She agrees that they have moved forward economically and socially, but she believes that in the process their relationship has become empty. So much energy has been devoted to material gain and career advancement that there is little time left for them to be together. Frank thinks things have never been better, but as far as Susan is concerned, things have never been worse.

Frank has depended on tangible signposts to mark progress in the relationship. But relationships involve many different domains, not just the material one. Frank does not know how to mark progress in the emotional and intimate areas of the marriage, so he chooses to ignore these. His experience in the business world has not prepared him to evaluate them.

We are encouraged to move on

Career advancement is often a series of strategic moves. If you're good at what you do, you will be promoted, change departments, receive offers from other companies. People are expected to change jobs as part of the advancement scheme. In some industries, changing jobs is routine; those who stay put for twenty years are the losers.

In relationships, however, moving on is usually perceived as a sign of failure. Few people are able to come away from a relationship breakup without feeling that they have failed in some way. Most people feel deeply hurt and even betrayed when partners move on.

There are, of course, people who are able to see the termination of a relationship as a normal way station in the course of life. They may even view a terminated relationship as a success—albeit one limited to a shorter duration. But by and large, the societal stigma regarding divorce and breakup is well-entrenched. In my own experience, people tend to be suspicious of advice columnists, marriage counselors, and authors of books on relationships if the advisors are divorced. There is a sense of "Physician, heal thyself."

In politics as well as in business, one occasionally hears the sentiment expressed that if an individual cannot take care of his or her domestic affairs, how can anyone have confidence in his or her ability to take care of the affairs of a business or a nation? Of course, there have been major shifts in these views over time, but societal norms do not change easily. Even in a time when divorce is fairly common, there is still a stigma attached to it. Just look at the words we use to describe it: "breaking up," "splitting," "getting dumped." Moreover, whereas it is acceptable to leave one job and go to another, it is considered unacceptable to leave one person for another. Saying that you have met someone else who better fills your needs is not taken as a sign of success at relating!

I sometimes give a talk in which I describe a relationship that has been unsatisfactory for a number of years. The wife, deciding she is no longer satisfied, wants out of the marriage. She still cares about her husband, but no longer in the same way. I tell the audience that, ten years ago, we might have said the woman was "dumping" her husband. But today we might say that she is simply "restructuring" the relationship. She is asking her husband that he remain her friend, but not her husband. Actually, such arrangements have become commonplace. But the audience always laughs when it hears about the switch in terminology. Why? Because when I say "restructure," they still hear "dump." Their views are that firmly entrenched.

When Jill decided to divorce Jack and "move on,"

she expected to receive a lot of reinforcement from the people around her. Everyone knew that Jack had a drinking problem and couldn't hold a job. Jill had tried to be understanding for five years, but it was clear that Jack wasn't ready to get help. She told her family and friends that she was going to leave him, and they were very understanding and supportive.

But once she had moved out, Jill received a rude awakening. The support she expected never materialized. Her friends, most of whom were married, seemed to distance themselves. Even her oldest friends, the ones she had known before she met Jack, did not make an effort to include her in their social circles. Her parents also changed their tune, warning her that whatever problems she had had with Jack, at least she'd had a marriage. Now she would be on her own. Maybe she wouldn't find someone else. They hoped she didn't expect to be dependent on their resources. They were retired and needed every penny.

Jill discovered that for all the fanfare about how society has moved forward and women have become liberated, the changes were mostly lip service. Society seemed remarkably unsupportive of her need to move on.

It is often not clear that this double standard exists between successful career behavior and successful relationship behavior. But the double standard has some basis. Fulfillment in relationships is achieved in a different way from fulfillment at work, and the goals are measured by different criteria. Rarely do people who move away from a relationship feel the kind of exhilaration and anticipation that marks their career moves.

We expect clear feedback from others

At work, you count on your superiors to give you clear feedback. But this is not so for interpersonal relationships. Most of the feedback you receive may be highly ambiguous. The personal stake you and your partner have in the relationship leads you to filter your responses and sometimes distort the feedback you do get. It is not uncommon in a relationship for a partner to find out that something is wrong only when the other person says he or she is leaving. The signs may have been there. But the feedback wasn't clear enough to enable correct interpretation.

When Allen asked for a divorce, Betsy was caught off-guard. She hadn't seen it coming and it didn't make any sense. Sure, their marriage had its ups and downs, but they had never talked about divorce. Nothing Allen had said or done had signaled to Betsy that things were so serious.

In fact, unbeknownst to Betsy, Allen had been seeing other women for almost five years. He had privately justified his actions by telling himself that seeing other women was the only way to keep his marriage together. Were it not for the affairs, he would have left Betsy five years earlier. But now he had reached a point where it wasn't enough to try to keep the marriage together by having affairs. He had met a woman he cared about deeply and he wanted to marry her.

When Allen announced that he wanted a divorce, Betsy thought about her job, where she supervised many employees. She knew that if an employee wasn't measuring up, she gave the person fair warning and a chance to improve before she fired him or her. Now she felt that Allen had "fired" her without warning. In fact, there had been many warnings that things were not going well. But they had been indirect, rather than direct.

The relationship between Allen and Betsy is a good example of the conspiracy partners sometimes engage in to cover up the fact that things are not working out. For example, their sex life had been almost nonexistent for several years, but they never talked about it. Surely Betsy understood this was the sign of a problem. Maybe she even knew or suspected that Allen was having affairs. But she said nothing. And instead of giving her clear feedback that he was dissatisfied, Allen pretended things were okay—until he finally couldn't pretend anymore.

In relationships, we are often forced to be detectives searching for clues. The feedback we seek is rarely found on the surface.

One person's gain is the other's loss

In the work environment, we are used to what are sometimes called "zero-sum games." That is, one person's win automatically becomes another person's loss. For example, when one salesman succeeds in selling a product to a customer, his competitor loses the sale. Or when one worker is chosen for promotion, another worker is passed over.

But in relationships, zero-sum games can be disastrous. A relationship cannot thrive as a competitive battleground. Win-lose games will undermine the relationship. What are needed are win-win strategies, where both partners benefit. Nevertheless, we are so used to playing zero-sum games that often our automatic response in a relationship is to think of our gain as being our partner's loss and vice versa.

Colleagues in his company refer to Victor as the "Silver Fox"—"silver" because of his lush, silver-gray hair, and "fox" because of his craftiness in getting accounts away from his competitors. In his business, computer maintenance, he knows there are only so many contracts to go around. Every time he gains a new client for the firm, it represents a severe blow to one of his competitors.

No one in the business questions Victor's success. But he has not been as successful in his love life as he has been in his work life. Perhaps this is because Victor tends to carry his work mentality into his personal relationships. He actually takes pride in outfoxing his lovers, just as he does in outfoxing his business competition. Victor would explain his attitude this way: He knows what he wants from a relationship, and the name of the game is to get it by whatever means necessary. It's no different than making a sale.

Because Victor is clever and charming, his strategies usually work—for a little while. But the relationships never last very long. Either Victor finds that he's not getting what he wants, or his partner catches on to the game. His relationships are basically short-term and selfish. Once he has "made the sale," he does not know how to offer authentic intimacy.

Work is task-oriented, not people-oriented

In business, there is a clearly defined mission or task to be accomplished. Interest in human relations is primarily in the service of this mission. If the employees are happy, they will produce more. But good human relations are not an end in themselves. A manager who does not perform will not keep his or her job unless the results can be produced.

We tend to carry this task orientation over into our personal relationships, and it is this factor that is responsible for many of our failures.

Louis is very good at his job as a middle-level manager for a company that manufactures automobile parts. He has successfully combined a high level of task orientation with an ability to motivate his employees to get the job done. He is a bottom-line manager who expects results from his employees, and when they produce results, he rewards them amply. When they don't produce, he gives them the opportunity to do better, but fires them if they can't measure up.

Although Louis knows that his skills at work are not exactly the same ones he needs in his role as Marian's husband, he's not quite sure what he should be doing differently. He is uncomfortable with the fogginess of role and task delineation within his marriage. When Marian complains that she just wants him "to be there" for her, he doesn't know what she means. He thinks it is a waste of time to concentrate on the relationship, rather than on their common goals and tasks. There is no visible "product" or goal to meet and he isn't sure what is expected of him.

Extra effort usually pays off

It counts for a lot when you put in special effort on the job. You are praised for going the extra mile, for working harder than your peers, for burning the midnight oil. But trying harder won't necessarily translate into success in personal relationships.

Vera has been trying very hard for six years to make her marriage to Tony work. In fact, the marriage has been held together by an act of will—Vera's will. But Tony doesn't make much of an effort at all. He comes and goes as he pleases and his addiction to gambling has put them in serious debt.

Vera often wonders, "How come things don't get any better? I try so hard."

But trying harder isn't going to change things for Vera and Tony.

Trying too hard can even be detrimental to relationships—particularly in the arena of sex.

Tom had had a rotten day at the office. He had been shouted down at a meeting and was being given signals by his superiors that unless he could control union demands, his responsibilities in the labor relations division of his organization might be reduced. He came home tired and cranky and had a couple of drinks to help him relax.

When he and Sylvia went to bed, he felt more than ready for sexual relief. But the harder he tried to get an erection, the more frustrated he became. Nothing happened. Sylvia told him not to worry about it and to get some sleep. But he couldn't sleep. His inability to perform sexually was the perfectly rotten ending to a rotten day. What was wrong with him? No matter how hard he tried, nothing worked.

The following day Tom was clearly out of sorts. Things weren't much better at work, although he was able to get one small concession from the union. But he was overtired and tense, and he felt that the union was giving him ground on the minor issues so that it could hold firm on the major ones. Tom was not going to have any of that. That night Tom and Sylvia went to bed and he was determined not to repeat the fiasco of the night before. But once again, he was unable to perform. Now he was seriously concerned that he was losing control in the sexual arena too. He tried harder and harder—until Sylvia put a stop to it. "Look, Tom," she said gently, "you're under a lot of pressure at work right now. You need a break and a chance to rest. Let's put sex on hold for a week."

Tom didn't like the idea at all. He was sure that he could lick the problem. But Sylvia insisted and he agreed. They didn't get through the week. By the fifth day, Tom was more than ready. Without any words between them, they started making love.

More is better

On the job, more is usually better. It's a very American way of thinking. But this notion does not work well in relationships. A relationship is like a seesaw, where a delicate balance must be maintained. More of one thing can throw other aspects of the relationship out of balance. For example, too much concentration on sex can lead to a decline in communication on other levels. Too much emphasis on friendship can get in the way of sexual passion. Too much "closeness" can feel stifling. Again and again, we find the need for balance in our relationships. We need to balance friendship with passion, our ideals with our reality, the time we spend with our partner with the time we spend alone or with others.

David and Sara had talked for years about their dream of opening a motel. They liked the idea of working together and they were attracted to the business of providing lodging and services to people. They obtained the bank financing that made it possible for them to buy a small motel. But they soon discovered that their business was a lot more work than they had ever anticipated. They plowed more and more of their time, energy, and soul into the motel.

When they started the venture, David and Sara believed it would nicely complement their marriage and make their relationship stronger. Instead, the business seemed to be devouring their marriage. One night, Sara commented that they didn't own the motel, the motel owned them. It had taken over their lives and was wrecking their marriage. They realized that they needed to restore a balance among all of the aspects of their life together.

Judgments are based on objective criteria

When you want to evaluate how well a person is doing on the job, there is usually a relatively objective record to help you do it. You look at the work, the number of merit raises over a set period, the history of promotions, the number of people supervised, and so on.

However, in relationships, no objective criteria exist. All evaluations are personal and people vary greatly in the criteria they use for making judgments. Truly, one person's meat can be another's poison in the world of relationships. With no objective standards, it is *perception of reality* that has the most importance. But your perception might be quite different from your partner's.

Connie had usually done things Todd's way during the twelve years of their relationship. She knew he had high standards, and she always tried to be everything he desired in a woman. But no matter how many changes Connie made to please him, Todd never seemed to appreciate how much she had achieved in her quest to be the right mate for him. He would often become moody and she could tell he was displeased, but when she begged him to tell her what was wrong, he was unable to give her a clear answer. She knew he was judging her harshly, but she could not grasp the criteria he was using.

Todd's controlling maneuvers were hardly the basis

for a healthy relationship. But as long as Connie sought rational explanations for unreasonable behavior, the relationship would not progress beyond its current dilemma.

Emotions get in the way of success

At the office, emotions get in the way. An angry exchange or an outburst of tears is considered unprofessional and will weaken a person's standing in the work environment. By the same token, a person who is too warm or "soft" might be viewed as not having what it takes to succeed in a business environment.

By contrast, emotions are the very substance of personal relationships. Much of the gratification we find in our relationships stems from the degree of emotional expression we are able to give and receive. Yet our socialization and our training in the workplace encourage the suppression of strong emotions.

No one had ever accused Natalie of being unemotional. She was a highly reactive person who seemed to be set off, either positively or negatively, by the slightest incident. Once she finished her outburst, the incident was usually over and she moved on. Natalie's personality allowed her to get things off her chest without letting them get to her. She was a generally happy person who didn't brood about things.

Natalie's husband, Sean, found Natalie's emotionalism irritating. He couldn't see the point of it. "Why are you crying?" he'd ask impatiently when they argued. "How does it help to solve anything?" Sean was uncomfortable with displays of emotion. He felt they blocked the way to a solution and were a sign of weakness.

Indeed, it is true that emotional expressions alone cannot lead to solutions in a relationship. But the ability to express strong emotions—whether they're positive or negative—is an essential element of intimacy. Couples who are afraid to let their emotions show are unlikely to reach anything but a superficial level of understanding.

The Golden Rule is suspended

"Do unto others as you would have them do unto you." That's the Golden Rule. Everyone swears by it—except in business. There we suspend the Golden Rule because if it were practiced, we'd never achieve our goals. We don't want our subordinates to treat us just the way we treat them. We don't expect our competitors to be considerate of our feelings and needs.

However, the Golden Rule is important in a personal relationship. Relationships shouldn't be "dog-eat-dog," but mutually supportive. Suspending the Golden Rule in our love lives can have terrible consequences.

Sol is a giver. Judy is a taker. Up until now, their marriage has worked pretty well because Sol has been content to give Judy what she wants and Judy has been content to take it. But now Sol wants something pretty big from Judy. His law firm is opening a new branch in the Midwest and he has been offered the opportunity to head it. Judy is East Coast-born and bred and she is vehement in her objection to moving. Sol feels that up until now he has always done things Judy's way and it's time for her to give a little. But the pattern has already been set in their marriage and Judy doesn't feel that she owes Sol anything. Long years of suspending the Golden Rule have created an impossible imbalance.

When we use the techniques of the business world to address the needs of a relationship, it can often have disastrous repercussions. Our workday ideology is poorly suited for the demands of our personal lives. This is easy to see when we evaluate the characteristics of the two:

WORK SUCCESS	LOVE SUCCESS
1. You can usually tell whether you are moving forward, standing still, or moving backward.	1. Growth is not linear; the status changes from day to day, and sometimes it is hard to know whether or not you're doing well.
2. Success is marked by steady advancements that often require moving on—that is, leaving your commitment to one job and making a commitment to a new one.	2. The inability to remain committed to a single partner is usually viewed as a sign of failure.
3. Our colleagues and superiors usually provide clear feedback on a regular basis.	3. Sometimes we receive inadequate or vague feedback, or we distort the feedback we do receive.
4. It is assumed that our success will be at the expense of others. The acceptable standard is, "May the best one win."	4. Success cannot be achieved at the expense of a partner.
5. The goal is to "get the job done." Sometimes this means sacrificing other things, such as interpersonal relationships.	5. Relationships are not task-oriented; the interpersonal dimension must be valued on an even par with other aspects of the relationship.

(Cont.)

WORK SUCCESS	LOVE SUCCESS
6. Extra effort is usually rewarded in specific ways; in many jobs, it is a guarantee of success.	6. Extra effort is not always useful, and sometimes it can be a detriment.
7. At work, more is usually better. Success is measured by the ability to accomplish tangible goals.	7. In relationships, the key is to maintain a balance; success isn't measured by "more" (e.g., "more sex" does not necessarily mean more love).
8. Criteria for success are objective.	8. Criteria for success are subjective—that is, they may be perceived in different ways by different people.
9. We are discouraged from showing emotion, or from taking action based on our feelings. Emotional responses are considered to be irrelevant.	9. Emotional reactions are valuable signals to what is going on.
10. We suspend the Golden Rule and are not expected to treat everyone on an equal footing. It is acceptable to make decisions based upon what is best for us (or the company) rather than what is best for others.	10. The Golden Rule is the cornerstone of success. Relationships require mutual support and empathy.

Relationship Intelligence scorns the rules of both the academic and the business worlds. As long as you depend on the knowledge you have attained in school or at work to handle personal interactions, you will continue to fail. In the next section, we will go into the Relationship Classroom and learn the techniques that will make you love-smart.

PART TWO

THE LOVE CLASSROOM

SIX LESSONS IN RELATIONSHIP INTELLIGENCE

L et's go into the Love Classroom and study the six lessons for Relationship Intelligence. Although we have discarded the techniques we learned in school and at work as being irrelevant in matters of love, we will learn a new set of techniques that apply the intellectual sciences to matters of the heart.

Some people balk at the very idea of learning how to love. They hold fast to the notion that if love does not flow spontaneously, it is not real. But these same people would have to admit that even the most loving relationships sometimes encounter crises that defy the romantic ideal of "love will conquer all." At times of crisis, they long for the wisdom to figure out what to do.

Many people also find the idea of applying intelligence or logic intimidating. They remember those impossible equations on school tests that left them so dizzy. But Relationship Intelligence is not an abstract science. It is a skill that can be learned by anybody. You don't have to be a "brain" to apply the techniques. You just have to be committed to making them work.

The lessons in Smart Love that we will discuss in the following chapters are not *rules*. They are guidelines. As such, they are contextless—that is, the unique circumstances of the relationship influence the way they are carried out. In this respect, they are quite different from the cause-and-effect methods that you may be familiar with from science and mathematics, or from the goal orientation of the workplace.

Very simply, Relationship Intelligence is the ability to make full use of your strengths and to circumvent or improve your weaknesses. It is the application of the broader concept of intelligence to the unique situations of your love relationships. Properly applied, it can make your relationships more enduring, more exciting, more flexible, more workable, more romantic, more adventurous, and more sexy.

CHAPTER FOUR

R.I. LESSON ONE

UNDERSTAND THE TRIANGULAR LOVE EQUATION

The beach was deserted and the cool ocean breeze brushed gently against them as they walked. John turned to Martha. "I love you," he said softly. He had waited a long time before saying it—waited for exactly the right moment.

Martha looked up at him and her eyes were full of feeling. "I love you, too."

That night, John gave Martha a ring. Three months later they were married.

Five years and countless battles later, they were ready to throw in the towel. The romantic moonlit beach seemed a million lifetimes away.

"If you loved me, you would care more about my

feelings," Martha accused John. "You'd want to spend more time with me and support me when I'm down."

"All you ever do is complain," he replied angrily. "I'm sick of it. What do you want from me?"

"Some affection, for one thing."

"Affection? How dare you say that? Lately, every time I want to make love, you turn me away."

"It's the only time you want to be with me. I need more than that."

"At least you don't complain then!" John stormed out of the room. A year later they were divorced.

This story is not uncommon. John and Martha may remain puzzled for the rest of their lives about why their relationship, so loaded with promise at the outset, fell apart. Their experience might make them cynical or overly wary of love. The hurt that comes with the dissolution of a relationship is a hard thing to resolve. What went wrong?

Perhaps it is best to ask: What is present when things are "right" with a relationship? What are we talking about when we talk about love? Is it a "feeling," a chemistry that draws two people together? Is it an overwhelming passion? Is it an understanding people share when they have common interests, values, and goals? Is it a deep and abiding friendship? Is it a decision to stay together, no matter what?

In fact, it is all of these things. In my Triangular Love Equation, I have identified three components that form the points of a triangle. These are the elements of the love equation. They include:

- Intimacy—the feelings of closeness, connectedness, and being bonded.

- Passion—the drive for romance, and physical and emotional attraction.

- Commitment—the decision that you love someone and the investment you make to maintain that love.

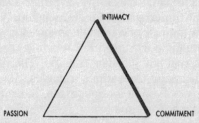

These three components operate dynamically, supporting one another. When any one or two of them is not present or is present in lesser strength, the love equation changes. For example, passion alone, without intimacy and commitment, is infatuation. Intimacy alone, without passion and commitment, is liking. Intimacy and passion without commitment is romantic love. There are many different kinds of love, and not every kind includes all three components or requires that they receive equal weight. Familial love, for example, usually consists of intimacy and commitment, but not passion.

We suffer in our relationships when we think the combination of components is different from what it is. For instance, a romantic summer affair may be exciting and fun, but the presence of passion and intimacy do not automatically imply a commitment. The element of commitment might be added later, or it might not. If you assume that strong passion and intimacy naturally lead to commitment, you may be wounded when your loved one moves on at the end of the summer.

Furthermore, not every component of the love triangle has equal weight at every moment. Your relationship may have more passion than intimacy in the beginning, since the bonded feelings of intimacy take time to develop. Or the components may ebb and flow over time. Passion, for example, is rarely constant in its strength for the duration of a relationship.

There is not just one triangle involved in a relationship, but multiple triangles. For example, each person has both a real and an ideal triangle. The greater the differences among the various triangles, the less satisfaction there will be in a relationship. In order for love to thrive, the actions in a loving relationship should reflect the size and shape of the lover's triangle. For example, if your real and ideal triangles are out of balance with one another, it indicates there is an imbalance in the relationship.

The Triangular Love Equation has at least two practical applications. The first is diagnostic. It will help you evaluate where you stand in a love relationship. The second application is therapeutic. Once you know where you stand, you are better equipped to make positive changes in your relationship.

Let's examine each of the components of love and illustrate how they perform interactively with other components.

INTIMACY

Intimacy is one of our most valuable human dynamics. It is the glue that binds us in common dedication and affection. It exists in any relationship where these elements are present:

1. Your desire to promote the welfare of another person.

2. Your happiness at being able to share experiences.

3. Your sense of regard for one another.

4. Your mutual understanding that you will "be there" for one another in times of need.

5. The core understanding you share that you are on the same wavelength.

6. Your willingness to give emotional support to one another.

7. Your ability to communicate on more than superficial or practical levels.

8. The acknowledgment of one another's value in your life.

PASSION

Passion is the romantic and physical element of a relationship. It is the easiest of the three to recognize, but that doesn't mean it is simple to define or control. Although passion is usually experienced physically, sexual activity also meets many different emotional needs. Passion can be described as:

1. Your romantic feelings.

2. Your physical attraction and desire to be together.

3. Your mutual sexual enjoyment and fulfillment.

4. Your physical and emotional arousal.

COMMITMENT

Commitment can be divided into two stages. The first is the decision that you love someone; the second is the determination to maintain that love over time. The commitment process is essential to every lasting relationship. It includes:

1. Your decision that what you feel for the other person is a special kind of love.

2. Your willingness to symbolize or articulate your love in some way.

3. Your understanding that the relationship is more than just a passing fancy.

4. Your decision to invest in the relationship for a defined period of time ("forever," "for the long term," etc.).

To better understand how these three components of love operate dynamically, let's first examine what a relationship looks like when they are not all present.

Intimacy alone: Liking

Daryl and Joan met soon after Joan ended a long and somewhat harrowing relationship. She had been involved with a married man and, after much suffering, had finally concluded that he was never going to leave his wife to form a full and committed partnership with her. Daryl had been divorced for several years and was interested in forming a new relationship. But Joan was still hurting from her involvement and she didn't feel ready to commit again. Moreover, even if she had felt ready, she probably would not have chosen Daryl because he was a supervisor in her plant and it was her policy to avoid involvement with people at work. Nevertheless, Daryl and Joan found that they had a lot in common. What began as an occasional lunch together evolved into a weekly routine. Daryl would have been interested in moving the relationship beyond friendship, but it was clear that Joan did not want anything more.

Eventually, both Daryl and Joan became romantically involved with other people, but their lunches and their friendship continued. They found that they could talk to each other about important things that were going on in their lives. Their relationship was intimate without being passionate. And although there was some commitment present, as there is in any friendship, it was not a clearly articulated or long-term commitment. Their lunches served an important function for them in the present. But when Joan married and moved away, they lost touch with each other.

Liking is the experience of intimacy without passion or commitment. By "liking," I mean something more than the feelings you have toward the casual acquaintances and passers-by in your life. You feel close and connected to someone without experiencing physical passion or necessarily making a long-term commitment. This form of intimacy is very common in the workplace. People who work together tend to become close, confide in one another, and form friendships. These relationships supply a necessary human dimension to the work environment. But outside the context of work, they rarely turn into long-term committed friendships or romantic partnerships.

Passion alone: Infatuated love

Josh was having trouble concentrating on his work. For an accountant, concentration is critical for performance and in the past he hadn't had trouble concentrating. But ever since he'd met Lois, a woman in his apartment building, he couldn't stop thinking about her. Although he barely knew her, he was completely infatuated and found himself thinking about her dozens of times a day. He suspected she was dating someone, but that didn't help him get over thinking about her. Finally he decided to ask her out. She refused him tactfully, telling him that she was seeing someone else. But her manner was mildly flirtatious—who could tell about the future?

During the coming months, Josh continued to feel obsessed by Lois. He often imagined them making love together; he could almost feel the way she would be in his arms. It was "love at first sight."

Nothing ever came of Josh's infatuation, and over time, with no encouragement from Lois, it went away. What he was experiencing, this feeling of "love at first sight," was passion without intimacy or commitment. He knew very little about Lois—certainly not enough to know what kind of partner she would make. But he had idealized her in his imagination, elevating her to the position of the perfect lover and partner.

Infatuations can arise out of the blue—with a glance, a touch, a word. They tend to be characterized by a high degree of bodily arousal. And they can vanish just as quickly as they appear. Sometimes people engage in infatuations they never act upon. Such fantasies, which almost everyone has at one time or another, can be healthy and even make real relationships grow stronger.

However, if the infatuation is serious and becomes obsessive, it can steal your time and energy from the other things in your life. It prevents you from engaging in meaningful relationships that are based on reality. Even if your infatuation leads to a real relationship, you're bound to be disappointed once you get to know the object of your fantasy and find that he or she does not measure up to your idealized view.

Commitment alone: Sterile love

Jodie has been married to Zack for twenty years. The first few years were happy ones. But after they began to have children, things started going wrong. Zack felt left out. No matter how hard Jodie tried to bring him back to her and include him in her love, he seemed to be jealous of the love she gave to the children—as though she were taking it away from him. Over the years, Zack continued to distance himself and Jodie continued to try to bring him closer. But finally she gave up. Zack's distancing had become a self-fulfilling prophecy. Jodie and the children grew closer and Zack was an outsider.

At times, Jodie thought about leaving her husband. But she didn't want to leave while the children were young. Later, as the children grew older, she found other reasons to stay. She kept hoping that things would change—maybe when the children left home, the two of them could be close again. But things never changed. Jodie and Zack lived together into their senior years, but their commitment lacked passion and intimacy.

Commitment in the absence of passion and intimacy is sterile. Its nature is closer to a contract than it is to being in love. In our society, sterile love is most often seen near the end of long-term relationships, when the partners have lost mutual emotional involvement and physical attraction. In other societies, where marriages are arranged, sterile love may mark the beginning of a relationship, and passion and intimacy may follow.

But when a relationship that was once filled with passion and a close emotional bond becomes sterile, it is very difficult to restore what has been lost. Often people wait for years for the "magic" to return, only to be disappointed when it doesn't.

Intimacy + Passion = Romantic Love

Craig was not very happy about the idea of moving to Brazil. But he had been asked by his company to set up a subsidiary there. He would only be required to stay for two years to get things going. Then he would return to headquarters in Los Angeles. It was a good career opportunity, so he agreed to go.

During his seventh month in Brazil, Craig met Maria. He had never considered Latin American women to be his "type," but Maria changed his mind. She was the first woman he had ever met with whom he could really share his feelings. The relationship rapidly grew closer. They fell in love and Craig, a confirmed bachelor of forty-two, decided that he could think about marriage after all. Six months after they met, he proposed to Maria.

Maria loved him and she wanted to marry him. But she was deeply committed to her family and culture and was unwilling to leave Brazil. She told Craig she would marry him if he was willing to stay with his company's office in Brazil and live there permanently.

Craig gave it a lot of thought. He was torn between his love for Maria and his dislike of her country. Finally, he realized that he would wither on the vine if he stayed. He just wouldn't be happy. The romance between Craig and Maria continued for the duration of Craig's stay in Brazil. Finally, the time came for him to return home. With great sadness, Craig and Maria took leave of one another. Both knew that it would be better for them not to see each other again. They were very much in love, but their life circumstances had led them to go their separate ways.

Romantic love involves intimacy plus passion. Romantic lovers are not only drawn to one another physically, they are also bonded emotionally. However, commitment is not a necessary part of romantic love. The lovers may believe that permanence is unlikely, impossible, or just an issue to be dealt with in the future.

There are many sides to romantic love. Sometimes it starts with passion and, as the partners become close, an intimate bond develops. Sometimes it starts as a deep friendship that, over time, grows in passion. But it is not necessarily consistent with commitment.

Intimacy + Commitment = Companionate Love

If you asked Mickey and Kathleen if they loved one another, both would say yes in a second. But they had found, in their seventeen years of marriage, that sex was not a very important part of their relationship. Neither had a very high sex drive, and they weren't particularly compatible in bed. They settled into a pattern of having sex only occasionally, deciding that they had so much going for them as a couple that they were willing to sacrifice the sexual aspect. In spite of the lack of passion, Mickey and Kathleen believed they were doing better in their marriage than most of the couples they knew. As they watched many of their friends break up, they felt grateful for what they had.

Companionate love is intimacy plus commitment. It might be described as a long-term, committed friendship. People differ in the extent to which companionate love meets their needs. Sometimes in marriage, passion subsides over time and is replaced by deeply felt commitment. Or couples go through periods where passion plays more or less of an important role. Companionate love might also describe the way family members interact, or be experienced with a cherished friend.

Passion + Commitment = Fatuous Love

Jenny met Tom at a singles bar. She knew that you weren't supposed to get serious about men you met in bars, but Jenny was wildly attracted to Tom. And he was wildly attracted to her. Jenny had not had much luck with relationships in the past, and she didn't want to lose Tom the way she had lost other men. After a very short time, she began pushing for a commitment. Tom was willing and, after only a few months, they were married.

By the end of the honeymoon, Jenny realized that she had made a terrible mistake. In the beginning, she had been happy that things had gone the way she wanted. She and Tom had been so terribly in love. But now she was finding that Tom was shallow and too willing to go along with whatever she suggested. He didn't seem to have any ideas of his own. In a word, he was a bore. Now that she had him, Jenny wasn't so sure she wanted him. She didn't want a man who just let himself be pushed around. In the meantime, Tom had started to resent Jenny's pushiness. He hated himself for just going along with whatever she suggested, but he didn't know how else to handle her. The relationship was wrong for both of them. It was still just a few months since they had met. But they were married. And they were both miserable.

Fatuous love is passion plus commitment. It is the "Hollywood love" that often includes a whirlwind courtship. It does not include the stabilizing factor of intimacy, which takes time to develop.

Fatuous love is vulnerable over time. When the passion fades—as it almost inevitably does—all that is left is commitment. But the commitment hasn't grown and deepened over time, so it is shallow.

Occasionally, intimacy may develop. But the expectations underlying the relationship can retard the development of intimacy. The couple expect a marriage made in heaven. They base the relationship on passion, but grow disillusioned when the passion starts to fade. They feel that they have been shortchanged and are getting much less than they bargained for. Their problem is that they bargained for too much passion and not enough intimacy.

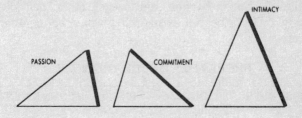

Intimacy + Passion + Commitment = Consummate Love

Jim and Amanda both knew that their remaining time was short. Jim's cancer had spread and the doctors had told them that at most he had a year to live. It was a bittersweet time for the couple. They had been married for forty-six years and had looked forward to reaching their golden anniversary. But now it didn't look as if this would happen.

Jim and Amanda had the kind of relationship that other couples envied. They had fallen in love with each other when they were young and they had never lost their love, even during the hard times. There had been a miscarriage. Once Jim had lost a job, and they didn't see how they would be able to make it financially. At various times they had gone through sexual dry spells, but they figured that happened in any marriage. They kept their perspective and humor, and their love saw them through all the tough times. Neither was religious, but they often said to each other, half jokingly, that if a heaven existed, they would be together there.

PROPERTIES OF THE TRIANGLE

PROPERTIES	INTIMACY	PASSION	COMMITMENT
1. Stability	moderately high	low	moderately high
2. Conscious controllability	moderate	low	high

(Cont.)

PROPERTIES	INTIMACY	PASSION	COMMITMENT
3. Experiential salience (awareness)	variable	high	variable
4. Typical importance in short-term relationships	moderate	high	low
5. Typical importance in long-term relationships	high	moderate	high
6. Commonality across loving relationships	high	low	moderate
7. Psychophysiological involvement	moderate	high	low

In my research, I determined that the three components of love have different properties: (1) Intimacy and commitment are more stable than passion, which tends to fluctuate widely. (2) It is possible to exert a great deal of control over commitment, and some control over intimacy, but little control over physical attraction or passion. (3) Awareness of passion is generally high while awareness of intimacy and commitment can be variable. (4/5) Passion tends to play a greater role in short-term relationships, while intimacy is usually developed over time, and commitment depends upon the long term. (6) Intimacy is common in most loving relationships, whether they be with lovers, family members, or friends, while passion is not common to relationships other than romantic ones, and commitment is only sometimes present in other relationships. (7) Passion is highly dependent on psychophysiological involvement, whereas commitment involves relatively little and intimacy only a moderate amount.

Consummate love is the full combination of intimacy, passion, and commitment. Most of us strive for this kind of love in our most important relationships. But the attainment of consummate love can be difficult. And keeping it can be even harder.

The Many Stages of Love

We view Jim and Amanda's "consummate love" as enviable. Who would not want such a deep and lasting relationship with another person? It's one of the greatest rewards of life. But even consummate love cannot be seen as an idealized state. Human beings are dynamic —they go through changes. Even in the most satisfying relationships, intimacy, passion, and commitment are not equally strong all the time. For example, when Amanda miscarried, she went through a period of private mourning that caused her to withdraw from Jim. She was unable to share what she was feeling with him. When Jim lost his job, he was depressed for a time and wasn't interested in sex. Now that Jim is dying of cancer, there is more closeness and intimacy than ever before, but little sex.

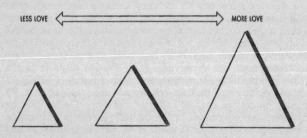

The levels of intimacy, passion, and commitment change over time. Sometimes these changes are due to the natural ebb and flow of a relationship; this was true for Jim and Amanda. Other times, the changes are more permanent. Because we tend to idealize love, we don't always recognize the ways in which natural changes can be signs of growth in our relationships. We panic and think something's wrong.

There are certain trends that are typical in love relationships. Intimacy tends to increase rather steadily at the beginning of a relationship, then at a slower rate. After a while it starts to level off. Early in a relationship, each partner is unknown to the other. There is a lot to discover. And each new discovery makes the couple feel closer. As time goes on, they become more predictable to one another and are no longer aware of feeling so much emotion or being as close. Sometimes this is a sign that the two individuals are growing apart. But it may also mean the relationship is thriving and the couple is growing together. Because of the steadiness of the growth, they may hardly be aware of their interdependence. In a successful relationship, deep intimacy will continue to grow while surface intimacy will fall off.

Passion, too, is often strongest at the start of a relationship—at least, the superficial feelings of passion. Over time, if sex is a constant in the relationship, it levels off to a less urgent form of passion. The urgency might revive again at certain points in the relationship —for example, when a couple has been apart for a period of time. But the absence of urgency does not mean the absence of passion.

The strength of commitment over time depends on the success of the relationship. The level starts at zero when a couple first meets. Generally, commitment begins very gradually, then speeds up. If the relationship continues over the long term, the feeling of commitment will level off and it will become a steady force. If the relationship begins to die, the level of commitment will decline. If it fails, the level of commitment may go back to zero or it may change into a different kind of commitment.

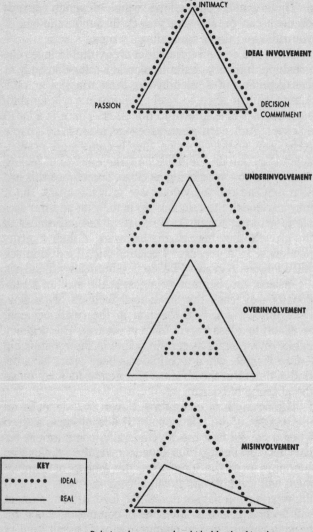

Relations between real and ideal levels of involvement.

The geometry of the love triangle depends not only on the balance of love, but also on the amount of love. If you think of your relationships as being a series of triangles of different sizes, the larger the triangle the greater amount of love you experience for that person. Less love is represented by a smaller triangle.

Real vs. Ideal Love

Each person in a relationship has both a real and an ideal triangle. If your real triangle, which represents the actual strength and balance of your relationship, is very different from your ideal triangle, which represents the strength and balance you desire, you're going to feel dissatisfied. However, some people spend a lifetime being dissatisfied. They excuse their lack of long-term partnerships by saying, "I have high standards." In fact, their standards are so unrealistic, it would be impossible for any mere human to measure up.

Geoff was thirty-six years old and eager to get married. But although he had dated many women over the years, he had never felt that any of them was quite right for him. He told himself that he had very high standards and that none of the women had met them. He didn't believe he should enter a permanent relationship with a woman who was not the person he really wanted.

Geoff was beginning to grow discouraged and he wondered if he would ever find the woman of his dreams. But he was unwilling to compromise because he knew he would always wonder whether he would have found the right woman if only he'd waited a little longer.

There are many people in Geoff's position—always looking for the perfect match and never finding it. They are afraid to tamper with their ideal for fear that a compromise will make them unhappy, but they are miserable in their pursuit of love because what they are looking for does not exist.

Your real and ideal triangles will not necessarily match those of your partner. In addition to what really exists and what you desire, there is also the factor of perception. You may perceive your partner to have more or less commitment, for example, but your perception may be different from what he or she believes is true. When we talk about "reality" in relationships, we must always take into account that reality exists in a framework of interpretations that are constantly being made by ourselves and others.

The Action Triangle

The Triangular Love Equation is not just a theoretical model for relationships; and intimacy, passion, and commitment are not just theoretical concepts. They are constantly being expressed by our actions.

Craig had assured Lucy that she was everything to him—that his life would mean nothing without her. At first, Lucy was very happy with Craig's assurances. She wanted a man who made her his top priority in life. But over time, Craig's assurances seemed to wear thin. Although he frequently talked about how important she was to him, Lucy didn't feel that his behavior matched his words. He traveled a great deal, and when he was in town, he always seemed to have things to do that took precedence over Lucy. She wondered how he could need her so much when he never seemed to be around. Eventually, Lucy decided that there were too many discrepancies between what Craig said and the way he behaved. She decided to leave him.

Craig wasn't necessarily being dishonest when he

told Lucy he loved her. But one of the most frequent sources of failure in relationships is the inability to express one's feelings fully in action. The action triangle represents the degree to which the various components are expressed. The actions that convey each of the three components of love differ. For example, intimacy might be expressed when you listen to your partner if he or she is down and offer advice, support, or even a hug. Passion might be expressed by behaving in a seductive way or making love. Commitment might be expressed by making promises or by giving a tangible symbol, such as a ring. However the three components are expressed, the actions will have concrete effects on the relationship. For example, feelings of intimacy, translated into intimate actions, will lead to greater intimacy. By the same token, feelings that are not expressed in action will lead to eventual destruction of the feelings.

Now that you understand the Triangular Love Equation, you have already learned one of the most important lessons about relationships: *They are dynamic*. The idea of "happy ever after" need not be a myth. But if it is to be a reality, you must respect the fact that your relationship will be in a constant state of change. Think of your relationship as a highway that is upgraded, maintained, and even rebuilt over time. It is never "perfect"; it is never "finished." In the following lessons, you will learn how to use the dynamics of the love equation to strengthen your relationships, to keep them exciting, and to upgrade and rebuild them during the course of your life.

The Sternberg Triangular Love Scale

I have often used the following scale to measure love and to test the validity of the triangular theory. It has proved to be a relatively good guide to determining the balance of the three components in a relationship. You can use it to evaluate the balance within your relationships.

Instructions: Consider the person with whom you are in a relationship. Rate each statement on a 1-to-9 scale, where 1 = "not at all," 5 = "moderately," and 9 = "extremely." Use intermediate points on the scale to indicate intermediate levels of feelings.

1. I am actively supportive of my partner's well-being. _____

2. I have a warm relationship with my partner. _____

3. Just seeing my partner excites me. _____

4. I know that I care about my partner. _____

5. I find myself thinking about my partner frequently throughout the day. _____

6. I am able to count on my partner in times of need. _____

7. I am committed to maintaining my relationship with my partner. _____

8. I have confidence in the stability of my relationship with my partner. _____

9. My relationship with my partner is very romantic. _____

10. My partner is able to count on me in times of need. _____

11. I find my partner to be very personally attractive. _____

12. Because of my commitment to my partner, I would not let other people come between us. _____

13. I expect my love for my partner to last the rest of my life. _____

14. I idealize my partner. _____

15. I am willing to share myself and my possessions with my partner. _____

16. I cannot imagine another person making me as happy as my partner does. _____

17. I would rather be with my partner than with anyone else. _____

18. I could not let anything get in the way of my commitment to my partner. _____

19. I receive considerable emotional support from my partner. _____

20. I will always feel a strong responsibility for my partner. _____

21. I give considerable emotional support to my partner. _____

22. There is nothing more important to me than my relationship with my partner. _____

23. I especially like physical contact with my partner. _____

24. I communicate well with my partner. _____

25. I value my partner greatly in my life. _____

26. I feel close to my partner. _____

27. I view my commitment to my partner as a solid one. _____

28. I cannot imagine ending my relationship with my partner. _____

29. There is something almost "magical" about my relationship with my partner. _____

30. I have a comfortable relationship with my partner. _____

31. I adore my partner. _____

32. I am certain of my love for my partner. _____

33. I view my relationship with my partner as permanent. _____

34. I cannot imagine life without my partner. _____

35. I view my relationship with my partner as a good decision. _____

36. I feel that I really understand my partner. _____

37. My relationship with my partner is passionate. _____

38. I feel that my partner really understands me. _____

39. I feel a sense of responsibility toward my partner. _____

40. I feel that I can really trust my partner. _____

41. When I see romantic movies or read romantic books, I think about my partner. _____

42. I share deep personal information about myself with my partner. _____

43. I plan to continue in my relationship with my partner. _____

44. Even when my partner is hard to deal with, I remain committed to our relationship. _____

45. I fantasize about my partner. _____

Scoring:

(1) Write down the number you assigned to each statement.

1.___ intimacy		6.___ intimacy
2.___ intimacy		7.___ commitment
3.___ passion		8.___ commitment
4.___ commitment		9.___ passion
5.___ passion		10.___ intimacy

11.___ passion
12.___ commitment
13.___ commitment
14.___ passion
15.___ intimacy
16.___ passion
17.___ passion
18.___ commitment
19.___ intimacy
20.___ commitment
21.___ intimacy
22.___ passion
23.___ passion
24.___ intimacy
25.___ intimacy
26.___ intimacy
27.___ commitment
28.___ commitment

29.___ passion
30.___ intimacy
31.___ passion
32.___ commitment
33.___ commitment
34.___ passion
35.___ commitment
36.___ intimacy
37.___ passion
38.___ intimacy
39.___ commitment
40.___ intimacy
41.___ passion
42.___ intimacy
43.___ commitment
44.___ commitment
45.___ passion

(2) Add up the numbers in the *intimacy* category: _____

(3) Add up the numbers in the *passion* category: _____

(4) Add up the numbers in the *commitment* category: _____

(5) Divide each of the three numbers by 15. This will give you an average rating for each of the three components.

It has been my experience that this scale helps people personalize the Triangular Love Equation and reach a greater understanding of the nature of their relationships. It is a good first step to Relationship Intelligence, and it is even more effective when partners share their scores. If you and your partner take the test together, use these questions to explore your findings:

1. What is your perception of the balance of your relationship (e.g., relatively well-balanced; passionate, but low on commitment)?

2. Did anything about your score surprise you?

3. What is your partner's perception of your relationship?

4. Did anything about your partner's score surprise you?

5. What are the differences between your perception and your partner's perception of your relationship?

6. How do each of your answers differ from what you perceive to be the "ideal" of your relationship?

CHAPTER FIVE

R.I.
LESSON
TWO

MAKE AN INVESTMENT IN CHANGE

Ultimately, Relationship Intelligence requires that we make some kind of commitment if we expect to reap benefits. It's a simple concept, and certainly one that we have no trouble accepting in virtually every other arena of our lives. The thousands of Americans who flock each year to Las Vegas or Atlantic City certainly understand that they won't win unless they make an investment. The stock market runs on this principle. So do most businesses. Bantam Books made an investment in me when it commissioned this book. The company paid me a certain amount of money in advance, trusting (but not knowing for sure) that I would deliver a manuscript and that it would eventually earn them back their investment, and then some.

Since it is such a familiar idea to us, why do we find the concept of commitment in interpersonal relationships so hard to grasp? Commitment is not an abstract idea. It is not simply *wanting* things to work. Nor is it *hoping* things will work. It is not even the *will* to make things work.

Commitment is action; it's "putting your money where your mouth is." It is an investment and, as such, has many of the characteristics that a financial investment has.

The greatest investment you will make in your life is in your romantic partner. Given this fact, it is amazing that so many people expect their relationships to yield them benefits spontaneously. They don't understand that you have to put something into the relationship in order to yield a return. Expecting results when you haven't invested in a relationship is analogous to expecting a return from the stock market without investing money.

All investments entail risk. Achieving a successful relationship holds the promise of great gains (or "return on investment"), but you risk losses as well. When you seek change and growth in your life, you are putting yourself on the line. You do not know whether your efforts will improve your relationship or not. You do not have a sure way to predict what your partner's response might be to changes you seek. But it's okay not to be sure. Risk-taking is a fundamental part of the dynamic of living.

Many people follow the ups and downs of the stock market and other financial indicators more closely than they follow the ups and downs of their romantic relationships. They are more likely to check the daily stock quotes than they are to check the daily state of their partnerships. They may follow the daily or weekly price of gold, but fail to notice whether the "gold" in their relationships has lost its value.

Before we discuss some specific strategies for problem solving and growth in relationships, let's examine this all-important investment. We can most easily grasp the concept of a relationship investment by using the analogies that are most common to us: those we find in the financial world. The same principles we use to invest our money serve as useful guidelines for learning to make an investment in love. The insight behind these principles can help us grasp the characteristics of healthy love investments and alert us to the traps we should avoid.

Take the risk

Not surprisingly, the first principle of investment success involves taking a risk. A risk is not the same as a gamble. Gambling is a blind action; you hope for a reward, but you don't perform the actions that are necessarily consistent with winning. The kind of risk we are talking about is reasonable risk—you have reason to expect that it will pay off, but you don't have a 100 percent guarantee.

Peggy has been dating Kurt for two years. Now they have reached the point of deciding where to go with their relationship. They have talked seriously about marriage, they have communicated their concerns and hopes, and they have agreed to make a decision within six months. So far, so good. But as the deadline approaches, Peggy finds that she is waffling back and forth on her decision. Even after all the time they have spent together, Peggy isn't sure that she really loves Kurt. She thinks she does, but she isn't convinced that her feelings are deep enough to sustain a lasting marriage.

Peggy must weigh the risks of making a choice about her relationship with Kurt. She is thirty-five years old and is beginning to worry about passing the point when she will be comfortable having children. Children are an important consideration for her, and she knows that Kurt would make a good father. She also questions whether or not her idea of romantic love might be too idealistic. Is she dreaming about a relationship that doesn't exist in the real world, and using that dream to gauge how good her relationship with Kurt is? These are some of the questions Peggy asks herself. She knows that, no matter what decision she makes, it entails risk. If she marries Kurt, she takes a chance that she will not feel content. If she doesn't marry him, she takes a chance that she will not find a man who can give her the things she wants—or that she will discover later, when it is too late, that she really wanted Kurt. Neither choice offers a guarantee.

There is no way to avoid risk in a relationship. There is no way to insure that the investment you have made will return to you the things you are seeking. Like financial investments, some relationships are riskier than others. But even when the direction you choose appears to be "safe," remember that there is no such thing as a totally safe choice in love.

The risks in relationships are of many different kinds—financial, health-related, parental, and so forth. Each of the general kinds of risks leads to more specific risks—such as, what might happen to love and its ingredients of intimacy, passion, and commitment? It is unrealistic to imagine that a relationship can exist without risks.

People who make financial investments know that, on the one hand, they can usually make a substantial gain on an investment only if they take a fair degree of risk. But they also know, on the other hand, that some risks are foolish and can result in their losing everything. When you practice Relationship Intelligence, you decide what kinds of risks are *acceptable*. That means you weigh the pros and cons of the investment, and make a decision about what you're willing to put on the line for the relationship.

Diversify your resources

Anna is enormously attracted to Ron, and she often imagines what it would be like to be married to him. Anna thinks Ron is a very exciting man, and they are great in bed together. Her concern is that they don't seem to share many common interests or values. Ron likes being outdoors and enjoys sports and other physical activities. Anna prefers spending her free time going to movies, plays, and museums. Ron is very dedicated to achieving financial success. Anna feels financial goals are not as important as personal fulfillment. Ron seems to have little interest in children, although he has told Anna that he is willing to have them. Anna loves children and she is concerned about Ron's lack of enthusiasm.

A fundamental principle of investing is diversification. When you put all of your money into one investment, you risk losing everything. The same is true for relationships. If they choose to marry, Ron and Anna are taking the risk that, should their passion decline, their commitment may not be strong enough to support their lack of intimacy in the many nonsexual arenas of their relationship.

Anna realizes that, in marrying Ron, she is not getting as much variety in their assets as she would like.

Their love life and sex life are everything she wants, but in other arenas they are incompatible. In the domains of values, interests, and marital roles, there are many differences. Ultimately, for this relationship to work, one or both of them will have to change some of their values, interests, and role expectations in order to make the investment more diverse.

In relationships, each of us must decide how much diversification or variety of assets we need. Some people find diversity by expanding their circle of close relationships. They seek different things from different people. This kind of diversification—"playing the field" —in romantic relationships can work for some people. But they risk having shallow and unsatisfying relationships for the sake of variety.

Use the past to predict the future

One way to predict the future performance of a certain type of investment is to review the past performance of that investment. This is called "technical analysis."

In relationships, an evaluation of past behavior is not a bad way to make some predictions about what future behavior might be. This evaluation isn't 100 percent accurate; since people and circumstances change, past behavior won't necessarily give you the secure evaluation you may seek. Nevertheless, long-term behavior patterns are rarely changed overnight, so they can be fairly reliable indicators of future behavior.

Karen keeps hoping that Harry's pattern of behavior will change. For reasons she can't understand, just when their relationship seems to be doing well, Harry will start seeing another woman. She might understand this behavior better if he had flings when things weren't going well between them. But she can't fathom why he would wander when their own relationship is so good. After living with Harry for four years, Karen has begun to recognize the pattern of his behavior, and she has held back from making a commitment to marriage. Whenever they have considered getting married, Harry's tendency to stray has made her reluctant to go ahead. And he has seemed content to leave the situation as it is.

After several sessions with a counselor, Karen begins to see that Harry subconsciously uses his affairs to create distance between them because he is afraid to get close to her. It is a pattern he has developed over a long period, and it is unlikely to change. Karen considers giving him an ultimatum, but she realizes there's no point. She may be able to change his behavior—at least for a while—but she won't be able to change the deep feelings that give rise to his behavior. Her "technical analysis" is that marriage to Harry would be a bad risk.

Often in relationships, we hope people will change. We even believe that we can be the agent of that change. And, while it's true that partners can encourage and support change, it ultimately has to come from within. It is a mistake to overestimate our ability to bring about change in others. When you are considering a commitment, your best course is to ask yourself whether you love and accept your partner as he or she is at that moment—not as you hope the person will be at a distant point in the future. If a person is not what you want and you can't live with who that person is, you have to assume that the person will continue in the future to be the way he or she has been in the past. And it is important to remember that, even if changes do occur, they may not be the changes you hoped for.

Respect the fundamentals

Sam isn't especially ambitious. He values many things in life more than he values reaching the top of the corporate ladder. He is willing to accept having less financially in return for the life-style he wants. But he is concerned with his wife, Trish, who has different values. While Trish has not been pushy about his career, Sam knows that the life-style she values can only be obtained with financial success. Since they have decided that, once they have children, Trish will quit her job for a few years to be home with them, the full responsibility for producing income will be Sam's.

Sam decides that he is going to place more focus on his work and become more ambitious in order to please Trish and provide his family with a better life-style. But after less than a year, his resolve is wavering. He is acting against his most fundamental instincts, and he finds that he is miserable. Although Trish has never directly pushed him on the issue, he can tell that she is not satisfied with their life-style.

In fundamental analysis, the future behavior of an investment is predicted on the basis of information about the investment that seems particularly relevant to its future performance. Sometimes the fundamental analysis is at odds with the evaluation of past performance. For example, while Trish has never pushed Sam to be more successful financially in the past, he has reason to believe, because of her stated values and preferences, that she may become unhappy in the future.

No prediction of the future is perfect. All you can do is to use the information available to make your analysis. In personal relationships, an evaluation of the fundamental values of your partner is a factor to balance with his or her past behavior.

Set your stakes

The more you invest, the greater the risk. That's true of any investment. Many people, having been "burned" in the past, are reluctant to invest more than feels safe in a relationship. That was the way Beverly felt. She was tired of giving herself to a relationship only to have it end and leave her feeling wounded. But Ev, who has been dating Beverly for several months, feels ready to make a greater commitment. He is willing to invest more in the relationship than is Beverly.

Ev has two choices. He can either wait it out, in the hope that, over time, Beverly will get over her past hurt and be willing to invest more in the relationship, or he can decide to lessen his own investment—or even end it completely.

In any kind of investment, there are two kinds of gains as well as two kinds of losses: the actual material gain or loss, and the psychological gain or loss. If Ev decides to end the relationship, he will experience both the material loss of no longer having Beverly in his life and the psychological loss of having his hopes shattered. But Ev might be heartened by the realization that there is something to be gained from virtually every relationship, whether or not that relationship is permanent. In that respect, there is no such thing as a complete loss in matters of love.

Evaluate growth and appreciation

When Celia first met Wendell, she had an intuition that
their relationship might develop into something serious. But three years later, Celia has less confidence in
her intuition than she did at first. Although they have
become closer, they are nowhere near where she feels
they should be. Now she is wondering whether the relationship will ever go anywhere or whether it might be
stuck. On one hand, she is reluctant to end the relationship—maybe it just needs more time. On the other
hand, since the relationship has been more or less
static for over a year, she has no basis for believing that
things are going to change.

In most of the relationships we enter, we have hopes
for at least some growth. At the beginning, we aren't
sure what the potential might be or how fast the relationship will grow. Moreover, we are aware that relationships sometimes decrease rather than increase in
value over time. Things may get worse instead of better. The same is true for any investment. Sometimes
even investments that seem safe don't turn out to be
that way. For example, we may get involved on a casual
basis and then find ourselves becoming more deeply
involved than we had expected. Or we may see a relationship leading to a serious involvement, only to find,
as Celia did, that it gets stuck along the way. We need
to be aware that there is the potential for both growth
and loss in any relationship—and it isn't always certain
at the outset which of these we can expect.

Find the dividends

We seek more than growth in our relationships; we also seek dividends. As in a stock market investment, it is possible to have growth with little or no dividends, or dividends with little or no growth. Ideally, a relationship would have both growth and dividends.

Erica is living a compromise. When she met John, she was very taken with him. She believed that the two of them had been made for each other. Now, after fifteen years of marriage, she laughs when she remembers how she felt. The close feeling she cherished in the beginning has all but faded now. But Erica has decided that she can live with that—the trade-offs are worth it. In most respects, Erica has exactly the life she wants: a beautiful home, two wonderful children, the time and money to travel, and the freedom to pursue her own interests. There was a time, in the early years of their marriage, when she wondered if she could be happy in a marriage that lacked true closeness. Later, she learned to adjust her expectations and to live for the many things she had in life, rather than regret what she did not have.

Erica's marriage has reaped many dividends, but has shown no real growth. Some people would find it intolerable to make the trade-off she has chosen. But Erica is very clear about the choice she has made. She is unwilling to forfeit the dividends for the possibility of achieving growth.

Does it seem cynical to view life and love so coldly, as a series of trade-offs? In fact, each person makes an evaluation of what he or she wants from life and from a relationship. Certain aspects of a relationship may mean more than others. For example, some people consider sex to be the cornerstone of their intimacy; for others, sex plays a lesser role. That's just the way life is. Should Erica be concerned that there is no growth in her marriage? Maybe. It depends on what she values in life. The decision to seek growth must be based on the understanding that it has a value that is greater than, or at least equal to, the dividends. In Erica's case, a commitment to growth may jeopardize the dividends she receives from her marriage.

Beware the options game

Lynn and Robert are waiting to see what's going to happen with their postgraduate plans before they commit themselves to a serious relationship. Both of them are applying for doctoral work—Lynn in biochemistry, and Robert in genetics. Given the scarcity of such opportunities, they don't want to commit themselves until they see whether they will be able to be together, or at least geographically close.

Robert is a lot more satisfied with this plan than Lynn. Lynn is confused about whether to put their relationship or her career first. At the very least, she wonders if one of them should be putting their relationship first. Otherwise, aren't they really just two separate, uncommitted people, involved in a relationship only as long as it is convenient? Even though they find postgraduate opportunities in neighboring communities, Robert and Lynn eventually break up. After the move, Lynn never again felt convinced that their relationship was enough of a priority that it could weather rough times in the future.

In financial investments, you can take out an option when you are not prepared to purchase a stock at the current selling price, but are willing to purchase the stock if the price becomes more favorable. You might take out an option to sell, as well. In personal relationships, we sometimes take out an option when we are not willing to commit ourselves unless some set of circumstances becomes more favorable. In Robert and Lynn's case, the circumstances were career and location. Both of them wanted to keep the relationship together, but only if all the circumstances were ideal. Ironically, when the circumstances eventually did work out, Lynn backed away from the relationship. She felt that it was a bad sign that they had taken an option in the first place. Many people feel this way. For example, a man may decide that he does not wish to marry a woman who hesitates to make a commitment until she is confident of his income level and professional standing.

When you take out an option on a relationship, you are attempting to reduce the risk by waiting to make sure the investment is favorable before you make the commitment. It's not always a bad idea. In some respects, taking time to get to know one another before making a commitment is similar to taking out an option. But if you place other values ahead of the relationship —such as money, location, and career—you have to question how much value your commitment has. To some extent, the love between two people should transcend other considerations. I once knew a woman who discovered a lump on her breast shortly after she became engaged to marry. Lying in her hospital bed before the surgery, she told her fiancé, "Why don't we hold off talking about making a commitment until we know the results of the surgery?" He refused, telling her that their love was strong enough to encompass every secondary consideration.

Protect your investment

If an investor buys gold or rare coins or stamps, he or she is likely to go to great pains to take care of and preserve the investment. People are sometimes not so careful about their relationships. They expect that, if love is there, their relationships will somehow keep going on their own steam. Or, sometimes couples are so focused on the act of getting married that they lose sight of all the things they'll have to do after the wedding to make their relationship work.

Carl was eager to marry Belinda, but he has done little to protect the investment he made in their marriage. Carl is very involved in his work and he resents it when Belinda asks him to spend more time with her or to share his feelings with her. He thinks she nags him. On occasion, he has said in frustration, "What do you want from me? I married you, didn't I?" He thinks the fact that he made the commitment to marry proves that he loves Belinda. He has no understanding of the need to protect and nurture a relationship over time. He is like a person who purchases a beautiful plant, then fails to water it.

If you give your relationship less than the care it needs, its value in your life is likely to decrease. Left unprotected or poorly protected, the relationship will start to decline in worth—just as would any other investment. And you may find that with care and nourishment, the relationship's value will increase.

Another good reason to protect your investment is the uncertainty of what investment analysts call a "random walk." Many shrewd stock market analysts believe that what occurs in the market is usually random—it cannot be predicted. In relationships, there is some predictability, but a lot less than most of us believe. The very fact that the divorce rate is close to 50 percent shows the inherent degree of unpredictability in relationships. We may lack a crystal ball with which to predict the future, but we can hedge our bets with the right amount of care.

Are You Willing to Risk?

It has been said that timing is everything when it comes to making an investment. This is true in love, as well. Every investment provides a window of opportunity—that moment when the situation is ripe for change or growth. How often have we heard people agonize over missed opportunities? How often have we listened to a string of "if onlys": "If only I had listened . . . ," "If only I had married her . . . ," "If only I had agreed to move. . . ."

Regret is a sad and debilitating emotion. It reminds us of the many ways we have failed. But it can be instructive if it also enables us to evaluate our past mistakes. Consider the relationships that didn't work for you—those you may have regrets about. Ask yourself:

- Was I willing to take a risk? If so, was it a reasonable risk, based on the information available?

- Did I expect one domain of my relationship (passion or intimacy or commitment) to fill all of my needs, and did I fail to develop a variety of shared values and goals?

- Did I listen to what my and my partner's past behaviors and fundamental values suggested about how we would behave in the future, or did I harbor false or unrealistic expectations?

- Did I ask myself what the implications of my decision would be in terms of eventual gain or loss?

- Did I encourage growth and change within the relationship, or was I paralyzed by the fear that growth would mean loss of control?

- Did I weigh the dividends against the disappointments and make a conscious choice about the value of the relationship, or did I make immediate decisions based on emotion?

- Did I procrastinate, wait, and hold out, hoping for just the right circumstances, or did I make choices based on my best instincts, even when I knew there was no guarantee?

- Did I cherish, protect, and nurture my relationship, or did I expect it to flourish of its own accord?

A successful relationship starts when both partners understand the extent of their investment and commit to do the things that investment requires. In the next chapters, when we talk about strategies to solve problems and enrich relationships, it is assumed that this basic commitment is present.

CHAPTER SIX

R.I.
LESSON
THREE

LEARN THE TECHNIQUES OF
PROBLEM SOLVING

Often in life, we have a self-defeating view of our problems, especially those that occur in matters of love. They can seem to overwhelm us and leave us feeling dizzy with confusion. We wonder why we have so much trouble relating to the very people for whom we feel the most love.

To be sure, problems that exist in relationships are not, as we have pointed out before, well-structured problems. They are messy and persistent—hard to identify and more complex to resolve.

But every person has the ability to be intelligent in relationships—given the commitment. Relationship Intelligence requires that we reach beyond our frustration and hopelessness to examine our problems and create a plan for their solutions.

Of course, problem recognition is the first step in the problem-solving cycle. A problem cannot be solved if we deny that one exists. Sometimes it's easy for both people to recognize that there is a problem, but that's not always the case. Thus, if you or your partner has started to behave in a manner that is both different and problematical, attend to that behavior right away. Sometimes small initial changes beget larger changes over the long term.

Each relationship is unique and brings with it a special set of circumstances, history, and attitudes. Nevertheless, there are some fundamental problem-solving techniques that work well as a starting point for negotiating resolutions in an effective way.

Let's take Keith and Tina, who have been married for two years, and walk them through the problem-solving techniques.

Put the problem under a microscope

Keith and Tina are in conflict over visits to Tina's parents. For Keith, who does not get along with his inlaws, the monthly visits happen about twelve times more often than he would like in a year. The visits require a drive across state and last the entire weekend. He resents having to make them. They take away from the little time he has to pursue his own interests, spend time alone with Tina, or simply relax. But Tina is very close to her parents. She is their only child and she feels responsible for keeping their small family unit together. She doesn't understand why Keith has to make such a big issue of this. She makes few demands on him, and she feels that this is the least Keith can do for her. They have reached a stalemate on the issue.

When people perpetually fight over the same issue, it is often because the problem is being defined by each of them in a different way, and this is true for Keith and Tina. Each of them is stuck in his or her own perception of what the problem is, and a single resolution, agreeable to both of them, does not seem possible. The first step in problem solving is to put the problem under a microscope and examine it from both points of view. The goal is to reach a common point of definition.

Set the problem in context

The first task is to reach agreement on the primary arenas in which the problem exists. This exercise helps to clarify what the problem is and what it is not. The external arena includes the actual physical circumstances upon which the problem is focused. The internal arena relates to the implications of the problem —how it is perceived by both parties.

PRIMARY ARENA: EXTERNAL	PRIMARY ARENA: INTERNAL
money	commitment
household	ideals
career	ethics
sex	freedom
extended family	self-esteem
friendships	sexuality
leisure	communication
children	respect
education	caring
religion	trust

It is important that Keith and Tina agree on both arenas. It is easy enough for them to do this externally; they agree that the problem is about extended family and use of leisure time. But it is more difficult to identify the internal perceptions. For Tina, the problem raises questions about Keith's commitment and the extent to which he cares for her. She asks him for so little —how can he refuse her this one thing, which is so important to her? She also sees it as an issue of respect. If Keith loves her, he should show respect for her family.

Keith sees things differently. He argues that he is completely committed to their marriage, but he doesn't think this means he should be forced to go along with things that are totally disagreeable to him. He sees the issue as the necessity of having freedom within a marriage to choose how he uses at least some of his leisure time. He finds the monthly schedule of visits arbitrary, and he reminds Tina that the planning of the visits went on between Tina and her parents, without his input.

In the course of their conversation, Keith also reveals another internal issue that Tina would never have guessed. He tells her that it has to do with self-esteem. One of the reasons he does not like to visit Tina's family is because he feels Tina's father always puts him down. On every visit, he manages to find an opportunity to mention something about Keith's job as a telephone company repairman, and to denigrate Keith. It's clear to Keith that Tina's father wishes his daughter were married to a professional, and their conversations make Keith feel tense and miserable.

Tina has noticed her father's remarks, but she never realized how much they hurt Keith. He has kept his strong feelings to himself. Now that the issue is out in the open, she finds herself having more sympathy for Keith's point of view.

By defining the arenas in which their problem occurs, Tina and Keith can begin by addressing one another's perceptions. Their conversation might sound
like this:

TINA: I think it is important that we stay close to my
        family, even if you don't like them very much.
        They're all we have, since your parents aren't
        alive. When we have children, it will be even
        more important. I don't ask you to give up your
        free time very often. Once a month doesn't
        seem like too much to ask.

KEITH: Once a month seems like a lot to me. In the
        course of a year, it's twenty-four days of doing
        something that puts me under stress. You never
        consulted me about how often we should visit
        your parents. I work hard and I think I should
        have a say in how I spend my free time.

TINA: I realize now how stressful it has been for you.
        My father's comments about your work make
        me angry. Why don't I have a talk with him, and
        ask him not to make those comments anymore.
        Would that help?

KEITH: Yes, it would help. But your father's attitude is
        only part of the problem. I still think that one
        weekend a month is too much time out of the
        limited time I have to relax and pursue my other
        interests. It also takes away from the time you
        and I have together.

TINA: That seems fair, but I have to consider my par-
        ents, too. They're not getting any younger, and
        I'm their only child. It means a lot for them to
        see me.

KEITH: But not necessarily to see me. Maybe you could
        see them without me part of the time.

In their conversation, Keith and Tina have not only articulated their own concerns, but have also expanded the issue to include the concerns of others who are not present—namely, Tina's parents. Very few relationship issues exist entirely within the closed circle of a couple. There are usually implications for others, as well. In this case, both Tina and Keith understand that their relationship with the extended family needs to be protected. They also agree that regular visits are important to Tina's parents—and that it is within the realm of their responsibility as a couple to take the concerns of Tina's parents into account. Had Keith said, "I don't care about how your parents feel," he would have been refusing that responsibility, and the problem would have taken on a different character.

Articulate the problem clearly

Once Keith and Tina have had the opportunity to share their perceptions, the couple must reach for a clear articulation of the problem about which they can be in agreement. This articulation is really an action statement, rather than a complaint. It would not be particularly useful for them to say, for example, that the problem is, "Tina wants Keith to visit her family every month and he doesn't want to." This is exactly the kind of statement that produces a deadlock. In making a statement about the problem, it is more useful to view it as a challenge that must be addressed, or a goal that must be achieved. Sometimes it helps to write it down to get exactly the right wording. This is not a game of semantics but, rather, an important step in the problem-solving technique. The way a problem is articulated determines the way in which it will be addressed.

Keith and Tina finally define their problem this way:

"The need to share time with Tina's parents, our only extended family, to offer them support and keep the family strong, without compromising our own needs as a couple and as individuals."

Their joint articulation of the problem takes into consideration each of their private concerns, and states them in a positive and action-oriented way.

Establish a consensus

One of the reasons that the solutions to our love problems often seem to fall flat is that we skip this step in the process. For example, a couple who agrees that their problem is that they don't spend enough time together might say, "Okay, let's decide that we're going to do that." They have moved from problem to resolution, without working out a strategy, and their solution (even though it is reached with the best of intentions) is an empty one.

To be successful, a solution must be approached openly and creatively, with the goal being to reach a consensus. A consensus implies that both parties can live with the solution. It would not be a consensus, for example, for Keith to dig in his heels and say, "I'm no longer going to visit your parents." In fact, were he to take this stand, the couple's problem would only grow worse. A consensus is reached when a couple acknowledges that the concerns of the other person must be taken care of in the process of deciding a solution. The first step is to brainstorm all of the possibilities.

Brainstorming is an open-ended creative process that allows all of the possible solutions to get out onto the table, without making judgments about them. Brainstorming can be a very enlightening process. It prevents the despair of feeling that there are no options available to help you solve your problems.

How does brainstorming work? Once you have defined the problem, list all the possible solutions—even those that seem impossible or far-fetched. This creative process is useful because, without the understanding that there are different possibilities for solutions, a problem can just hang in the air and fester. The brainstorming process requires an openness to listen and be flexible. A person who says he is "willing" to find a solution, but "only if you do it my way," is acting inflexibly and closes off the chance that a solution can be found. Keith and Tina brainstorm these possible solutions:

1. Tina's parents might visit them during certain months, giving Keith the freedom during the weekend to do other things in addition to spending time with his in-laws.

2. They might cut down on their visits, from every month to every other month or every six weeks.

3. Tina might visit her parents without Keith on certain months, and he would accompany her on others.

4. The couple might choose not to visit Tina's parents every month, but arrange to spend vacation time or holidays with them.

5. They might continue to visit every month for the time being, but agree to reduce their visits or consider the other options in the future.

6. They might reduce the number of their visits, but spend more time phoning and writing to Tina's parents, something they don't now do.

Each of these possible solutions takes into consideration the way Keith and Tina have defined the problem and, in a sense, any of the solutions might be pursued successfully, at least in the short term. Clearly, Keith and Tina are both willing to make some compromises. And the process of brainstorming has opened their eyes. Both now see that they do not have to be victims, that a number of options are available. One of the biggest difficulties couples have in reaching solutions is the inability to open their thinking to embrace a number of options. They see their problems in black and white with a narrow route to a solution.

Make a choice

Once the options are on the table, how do Keith and Tina go about choosing the best one? The method for choosing depends upon the type of problem they are addressing. I know a couple who uses what they call "alternation" when they are making decisions about their weekly night out together. They have different preferences, so they have agreed to alternate the choice. That way, each of them is fully satisfied at least half of the time.

Sometimes a "balance sheet" method is a good one. Another couple used this method when they reached a deadlock about the type of car they would buy. She wanted a Volvo and he wanted a Buick. After doing research on both models, they sat down and drew up a list of the pros and cons of each model, agreeing to go with the model that filled most of their needs.

Eventually, Keith and Tina decide upon a modification of the alternation method, choosing possibility number three, and also agreeing to approach Tina's parents about the first possibility. They decide that on odd-numbered months, Tina will visit her parents alone, and Keith will use those weekends to pursue his other interests. On even-numbered months, the two of them will visit Tina's parents together. They also decide that Tina will ask her parents to make the trip to visit them on at least two occasions during the coming year.

How does their solution solve the problem, including taking care of their individual concerns? Keith and Tina can check the validity of their solution by judging it against their articulation of the problem:

Does it meet the need to share time with Tina's parents? Yes—in fact, one or both of them will be spending the same amount of time with Tina's parents as they did before.

Does it meet their personal needs as individuals and as a couple? Yes—in fact, the new arrangement has some advantages they didn't even anticipate. Tina finds that the time alone with her parents has allowed a new intimacy to develop that got lost because she was always so busy worrying about Keith's unhappiness. On the months when Keith does join her, he feels less stress, too. Now that his concerns have been addressed and he is more aware of how important Tina's family is to her, he has made a greater effort to get to know Tina's parents as more than just adversaries. He is finding, to his surprise, that a more positive relationship is beginning to build.

On the months when Keith remains at home alone, he has enjoyed using the time to read and play golf with his friends, something he hasn't had time to do. Both he and Tina have learned the lesson that structuring time away from each other is a healthy thing, and it has strengthened their marriage.

Monitor the solution

No solution is ever written in concrete. As circumstances change, the solution must change to adapt to them. Keith and Tina's solution worked very well until they had their first child. At that point, they were less able to make frequent trips to visit Tina's parents, and, while the baby was small, Tina was unable to make the trip alone. At that time, they rearticulated the problem and negotiated a new agreement that included Tina's parents' making more frequent visits to them. And, as their daughter grew older, she often visited her grandparents for several days at a time while Keith and Tina spent time alone together.

When compromise isn't enough

By employing simple problem-solving techniques, Keith and Tina were able to reach a compromise that was agreeable to both of them. Compromise is an important skill in relationships. But compromise is only one way to resolve relationship problems. It's most often effective when the problem is a practical one that does not threaten the very fabric of the relationship. Sometimes, when the problem is more severe, a different method of reaching a solution is needed.

Peggy's husband, Brad, had engaged in several short affairs during their eight-year marriage. The first time Peggy found out about one of his affairs, she confronted him. He assured her that the affair meant nothing to him. "It was just a fling," he said. "It just happened. It has nothing to do with my love for you." He promised to end the affair, and Peggy forgave him and believed his promise that it would not happen again.

Two years later, she began to suspect that he was having another affair, and this time she felt devastated. She had believed him when he told her it wouldn't happen again, and now she wondered if she would ever be able to trust him. One night, after work, she told Brad that they had to talk.

"Are you having an affair?" she asked him directly.

He admitted that he was.

Peggy felt overwhelmed with sadness. She began to cry.

"Peggy," said Brad, putting his arms around her, "I don't want to hurt you, but you have to understand that these affairs mean nothing to me. I'm in love with you, not other women."

"But you don't think I'm enough for you."

"Of course you are," Brad assured her. "I would be lost without you. I think the problem is that you and I give different meanings to sex."

"I believe you mean that," Peggy told him seriously. "But I'm afraid I can't tolerate the idea that my husband has sex with other women. I can't stay with you if you're not going to be faithful to me."

Brad did not want to lose Peggy, and he promised that he would give up his affairs. But Peggy wondered if she could trust him. After all, he had made the same promise before.

Peggy and Brad were confronting a severe problem that threatened their marriage. Was it possible for them to reach a solution? Clearly, compromise was not the answer.

Defining the problem

Peggy and Brad each viewed their problem in a different way. According to Peggy, the problem touched on many arenas, including commitment, ethics, respect, shared ideals, and trust. It threatened not only their sex life, but also their whole identity as a couple. Brad viewed their primary problem as being one of poor communication and a lack of trust on Peggy's part. He insisted that the affairs themselves were only a problem because Peggy believed they were.

Finally, Brad and Peggy sought counseling because they could not reach a common definition of the problem on their own. After the counselor listened to each of their viewpoints on the problem, he suggested that they would make little headway unless they could reach a common understanding on certain important points. Specifically, he told them that they needed to check their perceptions of their real and ideal marriage and see whether they matched. "Right now," he said, "you are not coming to me as partners who share a problem. You are coming to me with two separate problems, and you're hoping I will pronounce judgment about which of you is right and which of you is wrong. Maybe the real problem is that you don't have a shared ideal of what your marriage should be."

Confronting different perceptions of love

Many of the problems that exist within relationships are caused by a gap between what one person thinks the relationship is and what it should be, and what the other person thinks the relationship is and what it should be. Unfortunately, most couples do not have the skills or the knowledge to clarify these important points early in the relationship. Often, because they share a common desire to see the relationship work, they make assumptions that they share a common understanding that doesn't exist. Brad and Peggy clearly had different ideas about fundamental aspects of their relationship, in particular, the importance of sexual fidelity. Peggy's view was consistent with the accepted public attitude. Brad pretended to Peggy that he was sexually faithful, but when she discovered his affairs, he expressed his real view: that sexual fidelity was not necessarily part of his marriage ideal. To Peggy, sex was closely connected to the components of intimacy and commitment. Brad believed it could be separate.

Is it possible for a couple who have such a major difference of perceptions to find a solution with which they can both be comfortable?

The couple's counselor suggested that, independently, they perform the following exercise:

Each of them was to take a sheet of paper and divide it down the center. On the left side, they were to make a heading, "Things I value about the relationship," and on the right side, they were to make a heading, "Things that bother me about the relationship."

After they had made their lists, the counselor then asked them to share what they had written. When they had done this, the counselor asked them to say how they felt, without specifically discussing the points on the lists.

Peggy admitted that the exercise made her feel less angry and threatened. "Seeing all the positive things in black and white made me feel better. And I almost didn't expect Brad to have many positive things to say, so I was surprised that he did."

The exercise was effective as a starting point in dialogue because it allowed Peggy and Brad to step back from their immediate problem and observe their relationship more broadly. It also allowed the opportunity for the mood to shift from "everything's bad" to "there are good things about the relationship"—something that's often hard to see when there is a deeply emotional conflict.

The exercise served as a good way to initiate a conversation about the extent to which Peggy and Brad's perceptions about the marriage, and their perceptions about what constituted an "ideal" marriage, were similar and different. Unless they could reach a point of commonality in their perceptions, it would not be possible for them to articulate a common problem, view it as a joint challenge, and act to find a solution. It is possible that their perceptions of the problem and their individual ideals of marriage were so different that they would never reach a point of consensus. But often the "balance sheet" approach to problem solving instigates a fresh dialogue that is productive. For example, in the process of revealing why sexual freedom is an important ideal, Brad might find that he is using his affairs to cover up certain insecurities. He might also admit that the affairs haven't provided him with much satisfaction. Peggy might learn some things about herself, too, when she examines her ideal of sexual monogamy. Without realizing it, she may have been using sex as a security blanket to hide her fear of losing Brad.

Relationship Intelligence assumes the willingness of both partners to use creativity and compromise to find the solutions to their everyday problems:

- They learn to listen with respect to one another's perception of the problem.

- They learn to reach a joint articulation of their problem that is clear and positive and leads the way to a solution.

- They learn to keep open minds as they brainstorm the many options that are available.

- They learn to reach a consensus on a solution that takes care of each partner's concerns.

- They learn to monitor their solutions and make appropriate adjustments as circumstances change.

Procedures for a couples' workshop

Every couple has a unique set of circumstances and assumptions that they bring with them to the relationship bargaining table. However, the following procedures are contentless; they provide the basis for understanding and resolution, no matter what uniquenesses exist. If you and your partner are struggling with a problem, and you are both committed to a resolution, these procedures should work for you. Use notebooks to write down your responses.

1. Individually, write down what you perceive to be the problem. In what external arena(s) does it exist? What internal arena(s) does it involve?

2. Share what you have written and discuss:

   - In what ways are your perceptions similar?

   - In what ways do your perceptions differ?

   - If your perceptions differ, what value do you find in what the other person is saying?

- What new insight do you gain by listening to your partner's articulation of the problem?

3. Using your statements as a basis, make a joint list of all the considerations that must be included in a satisfactory resolution.

4. Individually, write a statement of the problem, based on the list from number 3. The statement should be written as a positive action. To enable this, begin your statement with the words, "The challenge is . . ."

5. Share what you have written. Together, edit the individual statements until you have written one common statement that includes all the important points. This is the definition of your problem, which you are now calling a challenge.

6. Individually, make a list of all the possible things that can be done to handle the challenge.

7. Share and make a gestalt of your lists. A gestalt is an integration of points of commonality. When you have finished, you should have at least five strong options.

8. Discuss the pros and cons of each option and choose the one(s) that seem(s) most likely to work. (If you choose an option that doesn't work, you can always come back and try another option.)

9. Brainstorm together the specific actions that will have to be performed, then order them in terms of priority and timing. It might be helpful to use a calendar to plot out the time frame for each action.

10. Decide who is going to perform each action.

11. Select a date in the future for evaluating the results.

12. Symbolize your decision in some way. (This is a variation on the custom of "shaking on it" when you have reached a consensus.)

If this procedure seems sterile, believe me, it's not! The method exists only to provide a structure for your conversation and to keep you on track. But you will find the process invigorating. If you have felt defeated by your problems, you will likely experience a great catharsis as you discover that it is within your ability to resolve them.

The procedure also avoids subjectifying the problem. It does not include some of the debilitating aspects of many arguments, such as placing blame, making accusations, or downplaying the value of your partner's viewpoint. By the end of the process, both people should feel that their needs have been cared for, even if they have made compromises.

This is a true example of intelligence at work in a relationship.

R.I.
LESSON
FOUR

EMPLOY THE TACTICS OF SUCCESS

Effective problem solving requires more than simply following a step-by-step plan of action. It includes knowing when and how to make use of the help that is available in your environment. It may never have occurred to you how many sources of help exist. Pay attention to the following recommendations. They are the essential underpinnings of successful problem solving.

Make use of external feedback

Seek advice or observations from others who view your situation more objectively. Learning is a lifelong process, and one of the main ways we learn is by soliciting feedback from others. Often we are embarrassed to share our personal problems, even with our closest friends. Or we are eager to talk about our problems, but expect friends, and even professionals, to "side" with us, and we resent it when they make critical observations. But the objectivity of outside input may be the only thing that really enables a stalemated conflict to move to a point of resolution.

Spencer and Eleanor are having a hard time articulating their problem, but they are both aware of a great deal of friction between them these days. Neither of them feels very happy, and they seem to have trouble resolving even the most insignificant issues. It is clear to both of them that whatever is wrong, it transcends the quibbles. Finally, they decide to seek help from a marriage counselor.

After several counseling sessions, it comes out that Spencer is still struggling with an issue that he thought was long buried. Several years ago, he discovered evidence that Eleanor once had an affair with another man. He waited for her to say something about it. When she never did, he chose to say nothing to her, fearing what would happen if he brought it out into the open. Besides, it was a thing of the past.

Spencer thought he had pushed the matter out of his mind but, in fact, he had only pushed it out of his *conscious* mind. On a deeper, less conscious level, Spencer still feels hurt by Eleanor's betrayal.

All of these feelings are revealed during counseling and, at first, Eleanor says nothing. Finally, she admits that Spencer is right. She once had a very brief fling. "It only lasted a few weeks," she said. "I saw right away that it was a mistake and I ended it. I love Spencer. I didn't want to hurt him, so I never said anything about it."

Eleanor's affair had been brief, but the fallout had been blocking intimacy between the couple for a long time. It was all the more difficult to get past it because neither Eleanor nor Spencer recognized, on a conscious level, what was blocking them. Both considered the affair a thing of the past. But unresolved issues have a way of festering. They leave problems in their wake that are often difficult to connect with the original issue. This couple needed the help of an outside observer to shake loose their consciousness about the affair and bring it out into the open. It is unlikely that they could have easily reached this point on their own.

We would all like to be able to resolve our problems by ourselves. It is a humbling experience to admit we need help. We think, "If I'm so smart, why do I need to get help?" But ironically, the smartest people are the ones who know when to ask for help—and do so.

Listen to your internal feedback

Get in touch with your inner feedback, which is manifested in the reactions that come from your body and mind. Often, we can be so focused on the external feedback that comes from other people and from our environment that we fail to look inside ourselves. Sometimes the answer to our problems is not on the outside, but on the inside.

Gretchen is trying hard to make a go of things. Her husband, John, has an alcohol problem and, because of this, many of the family responsibilities fall to her. She is simultaneously trying to maintain a full-time job, keep the household running, and take care of their two children. To make matters worse, Gretchen also must take care of John and resolve the problems he creates because of his heavy drinking—including the abusive way he treats her and the children when he drinks.

Lately, Gretchen has been having trouble sleeping.

Even though she feels very tired, she tosses and turns throughout the night. As a result, she is even more exhausted and strung out, and she suffers frequent headaches. These are signals that something is wrong, but Gretchen doesn't heed them. She is sure that if only she tries a little bit harder, she can make things work.

But Gretchen's efforts are failing, and her body is screaming for help. It is telling her that she has pushed herself past the endurance point and she must let up on some of the responsibility she is taking for solving the problems in her marriage. If Gretchen were to listen to the warning signals emanating from her body, she would recognize the folly of her direction.

It is not unusual for people to ignore their internal feedback when they are in trouble, especially if they are high achievers who are used to asserting mind over matter to get things done. Many people hide their feelings behind stoicism, not trusting the validity of their internal feedback. "It's all in my head," Gretchen says, meaning it's nonsense. "If I could only pull myself together, I would be able to handle this situation better." In fact, Gretchen's body is "smarter" than she is. It is telling her that she has chosen the wrong way to resolve her problem.

Relationship Intelligence is the ability to consider all the data, not just the data that are immediately obvious. That includes what we observe, our perceptions of what we observe, and our feelings about what we observe. It is not unusual for an emotional battle to manifest itself in a churning stomach, so the churning stomach becomes data as well.

Check your perceptions

We are usually selective in the way we choose to perceive things. For example, when a partner is silent, we make an evaluation about whether he or she is feeling contentment or discontent. People who are relationship-smart learn to take all the pieces of information they receive from one another (including the "signals") and selectively put them together so as to make sense of the total package. They also know when they don't have enough information and need to seek more. For example, when it isn't clear whether a partner's silence is contentment or discontent, they might seek further information: "How are you doing?" "You look tired. Did you have a hard day at work?"

We are continually making inferences about other people's motives from their behavior. Because we do it so much, we often fail to recognize that our inferences are not necessarily accurate.

Jackie hasn't seemed to be herself lately, and Roy has been carefully observing her behavior in an attempt to figure out what is wrong. Ever since their son, Greg, was born three months ago, Jackie has shut Roy out. She devotes virtually all of her time to caring for the baby and is reluctant to let Roy help. He feels like a third wheel, and he wonders if he is losing Jackie's affection to the baby.

These are Roy's perceptions, and they may or may not be accurate. He has too much pride to talk to Jackie about his fears or to ask her for more attention. In his bitterness and hurt, he considers turning elsewhere for the affection that Jackie is withholding from him.

Roy's unwillingness to consider alternative interpretations for Jackie's behavior is driving him away from her. He wants to get even with her for what he perceives as her lack of interest in him. But if he were to sit down and talk honestly with his wife, he would find that her perception of the situation is very different from his own. Jackie is feeling very insecure about how to handle the baby. She is so worried that she might slip up in some way that she is afraid to focus on anything but the care of her child. Jackie has never forgotten how lack of attention caused her own sister to be injured when she was a baby. Her sister had been in her crib, crying and crying, but Jackie's parents had been busy in another room and had failed to heed her cries. Finally, her sister had climbed up and fallen out of the crib. She still carried the scar on her head where she had landed on the hardwood floor.

Without the data of what Jackie is experiencing, Roy's inferences are invalid and destructive. They could ultimately serve to drive a wedge between the couple that might destroy the closeness they had before the baby was born. It sounds so simple, and yet it is so crucial that Roy *ask* Jackie what she is feeling. Their dialogue, which should take place when both of them are relatively relaxed, might sound like this:

ROY: Jackie, I need to talk to you about something that has been bothering me.

JACKIE: Okay, what's wrong?

ROY: Ever since the baby was born, I feel left out of your life. Greg seems to take all of your time. I know he's a handful, but I'd like there to be a little time for us, too. You know, we haven't made love since Greg was born, and it's been three months now.

JACKIE (a little upset): I don't think you have any idea how much energy it takes to care for a newborn baby. I'm so tired most of the time that being romantic is the last thing on my mind.

ROY: I understand that, but when I try to help, you treat me like an intruder. I think maybe you worry too much. When Greg is awake, you don't leave him for a second. And, you know, my mother has offered to babysit so we can spend an evening by ourselves, and you've refused. I feel as if you don't want to be with me anymore.

JACKIE: It's not that, Roy. I would love to spend an evening alone with you. I miss you, too. But I don't want anything to happen to Greg. My sister got hurt when she was a baby because my mother left her alone in her crib.

ROY: You never told me about that.

JACKIE: She fell out of her crib and she could have been seriously injured. I'd never forgive myself if anything happened to Greg. I worry about it all the time.

ROY: I think you're overreacting. That's not going to happen to Greg. It's unrealistic to think you can watch him every minute. And you're making me feel completely left out. Whenever I hold Greg, you watch me like a hawk. Aren't we in this together?

JACKIE: I can't help it. Nobody ever showed me how to be a good mother. How should I know what's best?

ROY: Maybe it would help if we got to know some other new parents. There must be groups for new parents. Why don't we check with the hospital and Dr. Matthews and see if they can recommend one?

JACKIE: I guess that would be okay. I'm sorry if I've hurt

you. I really didn't know how you felt. Everything has been so confusing.

ROY: Look, Jackie, I'm sure we can work this out. But
I need to feel included. When you don't include
me, it really does hurt.

JACKIE (relieved): Okay. I'll try. I've been so worried
that I haven't been able to think straight.

Roy and Jackie have a long way to go in finding practical ways to resolve their situation. But they've taken
the important first step by clearing the air. As long as
Roy interpreted the situation on his own terms, without
checking with Jackie, the couple only became more and
more alienated. Now they have the opportunity to take
action in a positive way, based on their joint data.

Roy and Jackie are informally applying the problem-
solving procedures we discussed in the last chapter.
Every problem-solving effort, be it formal or informal,
begins with perception checking.

Apply your past knowledge

Your "new" problems do not exist in a vacuum. They
rise from the collective history of your other relationships. Use the lessons you have learned from past experiences and apply them to the problem at hand.
There is such a thing as a "learned response." If you
have discovered from past experience that a certain response is destructive, you can practice a change in behavior and make this change an automatic new form of
behavior.

But although it makes good sense to apply what you
have learned in past relationships to your new relationships, be careful that the lesson you think you have
learned is the right one.

David was married for eighteen years to a domineering woman who always got her way. He didn't know how to assert himself and it seemed easier to go along with what she wanted than to disrupt the fragile peace in their household. But eventually, he got tired of always giving in and being pushed around. He asked for a divorce and, after a bitter and prolonged court battle, he won his freedom.

Now David is interested in forming another relationship. But he is absolutely determined to apply what he learned from his first marriage. He will assert himself right away before things get out of hand. In this way, he can nip any problems in the bud. If the woman doesn't like it, she can leave. He's not going to get involved with a pushy woman again.

But as time goes on, David is puzzled about why it's so hard for him to get involved in a relationship. Women go out with him a few times, but suddenly they become too busy or too involved with other people to continue seeing him. On the one hand, David is proud that he is not letting himself be pushed around. On the other hand, he is puzzled about why nothing seems to be working out.

It might be that David has "learned" the wrong lesson from his past experience. In his fear of being "pushed around," he is going overboard in his effort to dominate his relationships right from the start. The women he goes out with are turned off by this dominating man who wants to control every aspect of their relationship. They quickly back off from him. Whereas David sees himself as avoiding being pushed around, the women with whom he is going out see him as seeking power and control.

What you learn is no good unless you apply it. But what you apply is no good unless you have learned the appropriate lesson. It might be said that David learned the wrong lesson—"I was a wimp, so now I'll be a bully"—and his attempts to apply it only made things worse.

One reason David became confused about the nature of his lesson from the past was that he simplified the problem, focusing all the blame for his failed marriage on the fact that his wife was too "pushy." We often oversimplify in this way when we evaluate previous relationships. The problem was not that his wife was too pushy and that he was too accommodating. Rather, it was that they were on different wavelengths and were unable to communicate their needs in appropriate ways. When seeking solutions from the past, it is useful to focus on where the communication breakdown occurred, keeping your eye on the ultimate goal, which is not to gain an upper hand, but to achieve a mutual respect. Consider the difference it would have made in David's life if he had articulated his past problem in this way: "I didn't communicate my needs very well. When my wife made demands, she had no way of knowing how I felt because I never told her. My silence and her assertiveness operated in tandem to create an atmosphere of resentment and mutual disrespect. In the future, I'm going to be more honest about expressing my needs. And I'm going to work on what it means to do that without being pushy myself."

Cope flexibly

Life doesn't stand still while you place a problem under a microscope. Your environment changes all the time, and the steps you take to resolve your problem have to change with the circumstances. Consider this example: You and your partner have decided to purchase a larger house, but one of you loses his or her job. It would be absurd for you to continue to focus on buying a house without considering how the change in your earning power will influence the matter. This is the tricky point when the process of problem solving often breaks down. One partner will say, "You promised we would do such-and-such" or "We made a commitment." Many people confuse commitment with inflexibility. Rather, commitment implies the extent to which you are able to adapt to new situations or make compromises in the process of finding solutions.

Things had gone relatively well for Jeff and Rebecca right up until the time they moved from a midsize city in the Northeast to a large city in California. They had made the move because Rebecca was accepted into a graduate program at a university in the city. The graduate program offered her a splendid opportunity to prepare for a career in molecular biology. But the way things were going, molecular biology was becoming the last thing on Rebecca's mind.

Everything about the city was a shock. The prices were too high, the life-style was too fast-paced, the people seemed superficial, and, worst of all, Rebecca and Jeff weren't getting along. Rebecca's program was very demanding, which added to the stress, and Jeff was having a hard time finding a job.

The stress of their new life began to show itself in their general behavior, and Jeff and Rebecca feared that their marriage was going down the drain. Nothing they tried seemed to make things better, until they jointly attended a three-day stress management workshop. At the workshop, they became aware of the enormous pressures under which they were operating. They also began to use the techniques taught in the workshop to reduce their stress. In particular, they found biofeedback helpful. A variety of relaxation techniques helped them cope and, as they began to relax, their relationship improved.

Relationships are inevitably affected by the environment in which they occur. If the environment is unfavorable, the relationship may suffer. Sometimes the problem is not really in the relationship at all, but rather in the couple's inability to cope flexibly with the environment.

Many different kind of changes can alter a relationship. The change can be a move, a new job, an illness, a financial circumstance, or any number of things. Relationship Intelligence requires that a couple keep adjusting their context to meet the changes that occur in their lives. There is a quick tendency to blame the relationship, to conclude that "we are falling out of love," while failing to take into consideration that the circumstances have been altered.

Avoid automatic responses

As we begin to get to know a person better, we often develop automatic strategies for coping with the various situations that arise. We learn how to handle the other person's moods, how to support his or her needs, and how to respond to the day-to-day ups and downs of life. But sooner or later, we may find that some of the automatic strategies that always worked in the past no longer work. There can be any number of reasons for this, but it's a fact of life. Because the strategies that have worked before often stop working, we need to balance our automatic strategies with new ones.

Beth knew exactly what to do when Abe came home a nervous wreck from his job in investment banking. She fixed him a drink, prepared him a hot bath, and rubbed his back. Some people might find this corny, but Beth had been married to Abe for twenty years, and she knew it worked, just as he knew what worked for her.

Beth had dozens of automatic strategies for coping with Abe's various moods. There was just one problem: Tonight it wasn't working. In fact, lately, as Abe seemed more and more strung out after work, Beth's method of soothing his nerves seemed to work less and less often. Neither Abe nor Beth understood why the things that had always worked in the past were failing now. Gradually, some of Beth's other automatic strategies started unraveling, too. As Abe became increasingly withdrawn and unresponsive, Beth grew alarmed with her inability to reach him. She felt very confused and uncertain about how to treat Abe, and she wondered if she had lost her ability to be a truly supportive partner. In fact, if Abe had been able to say what he really wanted, he would have told Beth, "I don't need a back rub. I need to talk."

We like to think that we "know" one another perfectly, that we have methods that will work for all time. Change can be discomfiting and make us feel insecure. But Relationship Intelligence requires the flexibility to respond in new ways when the old ways fail to work. Relationships that are not open-ended can become stale and make you feel that you are growing apart.

Shape your environment

Sometimes, Relationship Intelligence means that we take specific action to shape our environment rather than changing ourselves to adapt to the environment as it exists.

Dolores had tried to accommodate Ralph's ever-increasing demands for eight years. She tried to be just what Ralph wanted her to be. But as time went on, Dolores began to feel that she no longer knew who she was as an individual in her own right. She was in a nowhere-land, living in the shadow of Ralph's strong personality and aggressive demands.

Dolores finally decided that she had to take a chance on asserting herself with Ralph. One night, when he came home from work, she told him, "I've signed up for a class at the community college on Tuesday and Thursday evenings."

Ralph was surprised. "Why have you done that? It's pretty inconvenient. I work hard every day and now you're telling me that I'm going to have to worry about doing the household work, too. That's pretty selfish of you."

Dolores was determined. "You won't have to do anything. I'll make sure your dinner is ready before I leave."

"What do you think you're going to get out of these classes?" asked Ralph belligerently.

"I'm studying to be a legal secretary," Dolores said. "The children are grown and I need something for myself."

"I'm not enough for you, huh?" Ralph was only half joking when he said this.

"I love you, but you're not around most of the time," Dolores said.

"I don't like it," said Ralph, and Dolores recognized the threatening tone in his voice that had always stopped her in the past. But this time she would not be stopped. It was too important to her. She knew she was taking a chance, but she went ahead and started the classes. Ralph grumbled at first, but, much to her surprise, he eventually grew used to the idea. Over time, he even admitted that he liked the idea that Dolores would be sharing the financial load, especially now that they had two children in college. Elated, Dolores realized that now there was hope for her and for her marriage. She saw that it wasn't enough for her simply to adapt to her environment, responding only to Ralph's demands. Only by becoming a full person in her own right could she hope for a successful marriage.

Shaping the environment can be a frightening adventure. It means entering new territory and bucking the wishes of people who would like things to stay the way they are. But when you have tried adapting and it has failed, you need to consider whether the time has come to actively change the way things are. It is important to remember that human beings shape their environment every bit as much as it shapes them.

Accept your strengths and weaknesses

We all have strengths and weaknesses. Every person has things at which he or she excels. But being "smart" in one area of life does not mean that you are competent in all areas, for every person has weaknesses as well. We need to recognize our own strengths and weaknesses and those of our partners and learn to use them to strengthen our relationships.

Carol was at her wit's end with Chris, who was habitually late for everything. It was nearly impossible for her to maintain an orderly life for their family. If Chris was supposed to pick the children up from school, he was late. If he was supposed to take their son to baseball practice, he was late. If the two of them were going out to dinner, they were late. For years, Carol had tried to change Chris, but to no avail. She felt his chronic lateness indicated a lack of caring and respect for their family. One day, Carol demanded angrily that Chris come home early from work so they could discuss things. That night, he was later than ever. Carol was becoming obsessed with the issue of Chris's lateness and Chris, possibly as a way of avoiding his angry wife, was becoming less reliable than ever.

The situation would have been helped if Carol had realized that being late was a weakness in Chris that would probably not change at this stage in his life. Even his mother talked about how Chris had always dragged his feet as a child. It was time for Carol to ask herself how important this flaw really was. She needed to consider whether she would accomplish more by developing strategies to compensate for his behavior rather than aggressively trying to change it and growing resentful when change did not occur. For example, she might tell him that she wouldn't start dinner until she heard his car in the driveway. Or, if they were going to an event, she might tell Chris they were due earlier than they really were. These accommodations would ease the problem somewhat and would also relieve Carol's obsession with something that, ultimately, wasn't a very big problem in their relationship.

How do you know when to seek change and when to adapt? In one respect, the goal of a relationship should be constantly to seek change and renewal. But this cannot happen unless you acknowledge that human beings are imperfect. Sometimes we tend to get obsessed by a negative in the relationship to the exclusion of all the good things. When we focus on the weaknesses and fail to acknowledge the strengths, our partners tend to become defensive and perhaps even increase the negative behavior. No one likes to be repeatedly reminded of his or her inadequacies. Relationship Intelligence assumes that a quality of compassion exists between two people —the ability to forgive human failings and work together to meet one another's needs. The admonition to "lighten up" is not far off the mark.

These eight points form the basis of your mental check-list. When you are faced with a crisis in your relationship and don't seem to be able to see your way through to a resolution, it will help to refer to this mental checklist:

1. Have you made full use of outside input?

   —Have you sought help from professionals when it was appropriate?

   —Have you tried to find out about other people who have problems similar to your own (through groups, books, and other resources) and listened to their input?

2. Are you paying attention to internal feedback?

   —Have you noticed physical symptoms that seem to have no cause, such as lack of energy, headaches, stomach aches, inability to eat, or trouble sleeping?

   —Do you often feel anxious?

   —Have you become less interested in sex?

   —Do you feel afraid to say what you think or to express your feelings?

   —Does your partner seem to have something on his or her mind that is not being expressed?

   —Does your partner agree to things, even when you suspect that he or she would prefer something different?

   —Has your partner seemed unusually tense or anxious?

3. Have you checked your perceptions against those of your partner?

    —Can you clearly state your own perceptions?

    —Can you clearly state what you believe to be your partner's perceptions?

    —Have you asked your partner to tell you what's on his or her mind?

    —Can you identify places where your perceptions differ from those of your partner?

4. Are you listening to the lessons from your past?

    —Have you considered how your current problem might be related or similar to a problem that you have experienced in the past?

    —If it is, what might that tell you about the problem? Possibilities include: there is unfinished business from the past; you are compensating or reacting negatively as a result of past experiences rather than to valid concerns in the present; issues of this type have been consistently raised in your life.

5. Have you considered the recent changes in your environment?

    —Have you or your partner changed jobs?

    —Have you moved?

    —Have you experienced an illness in the family?

    —Have you recently become parents?

    —Have you or your partner started a new activity?

    —Has your financial status changed?

    —Has there been a death in the family?

If you answered yes to any of these questions, ask how that change might be influencing your problem.

6. Are you depending on automatic responses that are no longer valid?

   —Do you normally react in a certain way when you are confronted with this type of problem, or problems in general? For example, do you react by withdrawing, becoming angry, expressing hurt feelings, behaving in a compliant way, changing the subject?

   —Are there specific actions that normally accompany this response? For example, do you go out of your way to be pleasing, initiate sex, or give gifts? Do you refuse to talk, start a fight, or leave the house?

   —What assumptions are you making when you respond in these ways?

   —What might be faulty about your assumptions?

7. Are you failing to take action to make a change?

   —Have you considered the direct actions you can take to resolve your problem?

   —Can you describe the pros and cons of taking any of these actions?

   —Have you decided that you are willing to risk the possibility that the action you take will not work?

   —Are you prepared to take a different action if the first action does not resolve the problem?

8. Are you focusing on the weaknesses, rather than on the strengths, of your relationship?

—Can you describe the positive characteristics of your partner?

—Can you describe your own positive characteristics?

—Can you identify how these positive characteristics might be harnessed to solve your problems or improve your relationship?

—Are you overreacting to a problem? Ask yourself what its importance is on a scale of 1 to 10.

These are questions that should become a part of your mental checklist. They can help you become unstuck from a relationship problem. Relationship problems are fluid, rather than concrete. They can always be resolved, even though the resolution might take a different form from what you initially expected. Your mental checklist will enable you to lay aside your preconceived notions and will prepare you to take the appropriate action.

CHAPTER EIGHT

R.I.
LESSON
FIVE

UNMASK THE LOVE VILLAINS

Peer beneath the mask of a relationship, and you will often see another face entirely. The mask is worn for protection, to hide the vulnerability, pain, and fear that are at the core of every human interaction. We do not wear masks because we have bad intentions; often we're not even aware that we're hiding behind a false front. The mask is us—or so we believe.

I call these masks "love villains," because their presence in a relationship is the enemy that makes true loving impossible. Understand that the villain is not the person who wears the mask, it is the mask itself. Relationship Intelligence requires that we cut away the outer layer of falsehood to free ourselves and our loved ones to think, feel, and act without fear.

There are many kinds of masked characters in the world. But some appear as regular villains in our love dramas. They include: The Controller, the Typecaster, the Pious Fraud, the Procrastinator, the Conflict Avoider, the Yes-Sayer, the Expert, the Righteous Accuser, the Pretender, and the Blamer.

When we learn to recognize the person beneath the mask, and to listen to the real message being communicated by his or her behavior, suddenly we discover options for fulfillment within our relationships that we never thought possible.

Observe the characteristics of the masked villains, and see if you recognize them in yourself or in those you love.

MASK:	The Controller
OVERT MESSAGE:	"You are so incompetent or unreasonable that I am forced to take charge."
HIDDEN MESSAGE:	"I am afraid that if I don't keep you in line, you might do something to hurt me. I have to control you or I might lose you."
LESSON:	Winning by intimidation is not winning at all, especially in the realm of interpersonal relationships. Intimidation can take many forms; it can be physical abuse or mental abuse. It is a show of strength by one person over another—in other words, bullying. A person who gets his or her way by using intimidation is really interested in controlling the relationship—usually out of fear of what might happen if the control is loosened. This person may think that intimidation works, since it often provides an immediate

resolution. But a resolution that has its roots in fear or oneupmanship will ultimately be destructive.

An intimidator may justify the behavior by saying the partner deserved it, or by saying, "You pushed me so hard that I had no choice." Intimidators seek many justifications for their actions; over time, they learn to view their actions as entirely appropriate. The person who is intimidated may go along for a while and accept the blame, or at least learn to hide behavior that might bring out the bully. But eventually, a person who is repeatedly intimidated will reach a breaking point.

Warren doesn't remember the first time he hit Jana. But Jana remembers. They were having a heated argument about Warren's failure to perform certain household tasks. Warren claimed that since his job brought in most of the family's income, Jana should not expect him to work around the house, too. Jana held her ground, even as Warren became increasingly worked up. Then, to Jana's utter amazement, he slapped her. Warren had never hit her before and Jana was shocked and hurt. She quickly backed down and retreated to another room. Warren did not consider himself to be a violent man, but he learned that when Jana got really obstinate, a little display of physical force could get some sense into her head. Over the years, he occasionally struck his wife and, when he did, she always became agreeable. Eventually, she stopped arguing with him because she feared the possibility of violence.

Now Warren thinks the problem is solved—that Jana has finally learned to behave in a sensible fashion. But Jana's silence is the result of intimidation, not agreement. She is biding her time until she has saved up enough money to make it on her own. Then she plans to leave Warren.

A more subtle form of intimidation occurs when one partner belittles the other. A solid relationship must be built on a foundation of respect—both for oneself and for one's partner. Belittling your partner will undermine the relationship. If you value getting your way more than you value your relationship, there is no chance that you will ever reach the point of mutual respect that is essential to growth.

Scott grew up in a tough neighborhood and, through necessity, he became a master of the verbal jab. He now uses his finely honed skill in verbal combat with his lover, Roseann. Scott doesn't negotiate. He doesn't even argue. He ridicules. He gets his way by making Roseann feel so small and insignificant that she will go along with what he wants.

Roseann does not have Scott's verbal facility and she doesn't know how to respond. Over time, Scott's constant clever putdowns begin to undermine Roseann's self-esteem. She feels stupid and clumsy. Indeed, Scott may win his battles with Roseann, but his victory is an empty one, since he will ultimately lose Roseann's trust and good will.

If you are in a relationship in which you are the belittler, ask yourself whether the goal of getting your way justifies the ultimate breakdown of trust and respect. If you are the person who is belittled, ask yourself whether you are allowing the dynamic to continue by behaving in a submissive way—even agreeing that the belittlement is justified. Belittlement is never justified. It is the enemy of love and respect.

MASK:	The Typecaster
OVERT MESSAGE:	"The problem with my last relationship was that I chose the wrong kind of person."
HIDDEN MESSAGE:	"I am not responsible for the success

or failure of my relationships; it depends on the type of person I choose."

LESSON: Sometimes, when a relationship has failed, it is easy to place the blame on the other person. Then, the tendency is to look for a new relationship that will provide everything that was missing in the last one. If you're on the rebound from an especially traumatic relationship, you are especially susceptible to a form of typecasting that leads you to seek out the opposite extreme.

Melanie had recently ended a relationship with "Mr. Wrong." The way she described it, "I came to see that Eric embodied everything I despised. He was into money, power, and getting ahead no matter what it cost other people." Determined to learn from her mistake, Melanie started looking for a man who was as different from Eric as possible. Two months after she broke up with him, she met Arthur. She quickly saw that he was everything that Eric had not been. Arthur seemed so gentle. He was not into earning a lot of money or being aggressive about getting ahead. Melanie was convinced that she had learned from her mistake, and she felt lucky to meet someone like Arthur.

But a year later, Melanie was convinced that she had made a serious mistake. The relationship was going nowhere, and Arthur was going nowhere as well. He was not succeeding in his work, and he seemed oddly proud of the fact. He often bragged to Melanie about how he would never "sell out." He worked only intermittently, and was constantly out of money. When Melanie asked him questions about his goals, he would say,

"It's not what you do, it's who you are." Melanie was beginning to see that, in her desire to escape Eric's manic world, she had chosen the other extreme. Both were unacceptable to her.

Trading in one relationship for another that is its opposite is a way of refusing to take responsibility for your role in a relationship. It is also a way of assigning characteristics to people and labeling them in a way that meets your approval or disapproval. Another way this shows up is when people make universal assumptions about another person, based on that person's behavior in one situation.

It took Stan ten months after he met Jennifer, a secretary in his company, to ask her out. When he first met her, Stan thought Jennifer was very attractive, but he hesitated to approach her because she seemed very formal and just a little bit too correct for his taste. In other words, Stan didn't think Jennifer was his "type."

After nearly a year had passed, Stan asked Jennifer out on a whim, not really expecting things to work well between them. But to his surprise, he found Jennifer to be an extremely warm and interesting person, who demonstrated none of the formality she used at the office. When he mentioned the difference, Jennifer explained that what he took for coolness at work was only her way of being efficient and effective while she was trying to learn the ropes.

Sometimes behavior in one situation is representative of behavior in other situations. But often it is not. In any case, when we typecast people, we lose the opportunity to know and appreciate them.

MASK: The Pious Fraud
OVERT MESSAGE: "I have legitimate reasons for behaving the way I do. But your behavior is caused by character flaws."

HIDDEN MESSAGE: "If there are conflicts in our relationship, they're not really my fault."

LESSON: Sometimes we're unaware of the extent to which we may use a double standard in judging our own and our partner's actions. For example, we might consider our own behavior to be the result of outside influences ("My boss is putting a lot of pressure on me"). But we attribute comparable behavior in our partner to his or her inherent character.

Tammy felt that Al was just plain hostile toward her. His hostility showed in the number of fights they had. It seemed that scarcely a day would go by when they weren't arguing, and, although she loved Al, Tammy's idea of a good relationship did not include constant fighting. And she could not understand why Al felt so hostile toward her. When *she* argued with *him,* she always had a legitimate reason. He seemed to erupt without reason.

If you talked to Al, a very different story emerged. He agreed that he and Tammy were constantly fighting, and he was as distressed by the fights as Tammy was. But, according to Al, Tammy was the hostile one. He said, "If I seem hostile, it's only because I'm responding to her in kind."

Nobody's perfect, and most of us are willing to admit that we have imperfections. But it is common for people to attribute their own faults to situational factors, while judging the weaknesses of others as being due to flaws in their basic character.

You can recognize the mask of the Pious Fraud by examining your justifications. If you constantly feel like the victim of another person's actions, or believe you are being unfairly accused, these responses are clues that you are denying your own responsibility for the problem.

MASK:	The Procrastinator
OVERT MESSAGE:	"It's better to be safe than sorry."
HIDDEN MESSAGE:	"I'm afraid of what will happen if I make the wrong decision."
LESSON:	There are times when it makes sense to adopt a wait-and-see attitude, because the evidence needed to reach a resolution is not yet available. But there is a big difference between taking a wait-and-see attitude and putting off making a decision because you're afraid of committing yourself to a definite course of action. If you honestly believe that all of the information needed to make a decision is not in, you must take action to collect the information. Passively waiting for an undetermined time in the future when you will know better or feel more secure is only a delaying tactic that will lead to further friction rather than resolution. If one or both partners consistently put off making important decisions, the relationship will stagnate.

Cheryl believes that she and Brian are wasting money on rent, and she wants to buy a house. Brian is reluctant to move. He agrees that a house would be a better financial investment, but the idea makes him fearful. Buying a house is a big responsibility and Brian is not sure he's ready for it. He asks Cheryl to postpone the issue for a little while until he gets more settled in his new job. Cheryl agrees, but the "little while" turns into two years and they seem to be no closer than ever to buying a house. Cheryl is fed up with Brian. It now seems clear that his procrastination might be indefinite.

Sometimes all that is needed to unmask the Procrastinator is to set a deadline. Cheryl might say to Brian, "Let's choose a date by which time we will have made a decision." If Brian refuses, Cheryl can make an ultimatum—if she's sure she can abide by it.

MASK:	The Conflict Avoider
OVERT MESSAGE:	"I don't see a problem."
HIDDEN MESSAGE:	"If we start talking about this problem, I might end up having to make embarrassing admissions."
LESSON:	Denial is a strategy of conflict avoidance, not conflict resolution. Pretending a conflict does not exist will not make it go away. Often in relationships, one partner will fail to acknowledge the validity of the other's concerns. But if one person is distressed about a particular situation, then that situation becomes an issue for the relationship.

Dean has been overcharging his business clients, and Ruth has found out about it. It disturbs her a great deal, and she wants to discuss it with Dean. But every time she tries to approach him about it, he changes the subject or moves away. He refuses to recognize that his overcharging of clients has become a problem between him and Ruth. As far as he is concerned, business matters should be separate from personal issues. He doesn't want to mix the two. But Ruth doesn't think the two can be separated when it comes to matters of personal integrity. She thinks Dean's business cheating and his subsequent refusal to deal with it openly and honestly are creating unbearable friction in their marriage. She has become disillusioned with him, and she wonders how honest he has been with her in the past.

Denial is one of the hardest masks to crack; it is complete closure. Denial can lead to all kinds of additional problems. When your partner cuts you off at the pass, it is tempting to use threats, seek revenge, or subvert the person's actions in some way. These responses will only make matters worse. There is no way to force a Conflict Avoider to move past denial. All you can do is let the person know how you feel, and make it clear that you won't love him or her any less for being honest. In fact, honesty will strengthen your relationship, not weaken it.

MASK:	The Yes-Sayer
OVERT MESSAGE:	"If I give in just one more time, this will be the time when things work out."
HIDDEN MESSAGE:	"I'm afraid that if I don't give in, you'll leave me."
LESSON:	Lisa was packing her bags, preparing to move with her husband, Rick, to yet another city—their fifth move in as many years. The last time they moved, Lisa had promised herself that it was the last time. But here she was, agreeing to move again. Rick was very persuasive, as he described to her the ways that making yet another move would help him fulfill his

ambitions. "I don't like these moves any more than you do," he told Lisa. "But it's the only way to get ahead. Once I get into top management, we won't have to move anymore." Lisa had heard the story before. Every time they moved, Rick said it looked as if this would be the position that would finally propel him to the top.

In the meantime, Lisa's own career as a teacher had been on hold; with the annual move, the best she could do was to get substitute teaching jobs. Sometimes Lisa felt resentful, but ultimately she decided to keep moving with Rick, because the indications were always there that the next job would be the one that would allow him to have some stability.

Lisa was committing the "Chamberlain fallacy," which is the belief that if you give in to another person just one more time, a new pattern of behavior will emerge. The fallacy is named after the British Prime Minister, Neville Chamberlain, who repeatedly appeased Hitler before World War II. Chamberlain falsely believed that if he just made one more concession to Hitler, Hitler would be satisfied. The outcome of this fallacy is history.

Lisa was making the same mistake. Given Rick's past pattern, she had no reason to believe that things would change. Moreover, she had made unreasonable sacrifices of her own career fulfillment in order to appease Rick.

Compliance is usually practiced as a way of keeping the peace. There is always the expectation by the compliant one that, in the long run, it makes more sense to give in than to make waves.

Compliant people are usually matched with partners

who are aggressive and persistent. This was true of Leah and Roger. Leah had always found that if she was persistent enough, she could get anything she wanted. She was now applying the same strategies in her marriage, and they seemed to be working. Roger used to fight back when he disagreed with her, but eventually, he found that it was easier to just go along. Each time he did this, he hoped that it would be the turning point, the time when Leah was finally satisfied.

There's give-and-take in every relationship, but when one person does all the giving in, it is an unhealthy sign for a relationship. Yes, the peace may be kept, but at what price? Without meaningful dialogue, the intimacy that is the foundation of a good relationship is eventually destroyed.

If you are in a relationship where you do all the giving in, you need to learn to negotiate your rights. Sometimes that means you have to just say no, and force your partner to take you seriously. Don't kid yourself that you are simply an "agreeable" person, or that there is value in keeping the peace. If you examine your feelings carefully, you'll find that, deep down, you are probably harboring many resentments. Sooner or later, these will lead to a breakdown in the relationship. In fact, it is not uncommon for a Yes-Sayer eventually to crack after years of giving in. The "last straw" syndrome—expressing twenty years' worth of anger over one incident—has been fatal to many couples.

MASK:	The Expert
OVERT MESSAGE:	"I know what's best."
HIDDEN MESSAGE:	"I don't want to listen to you, because I want my way, no matter what you say."
LESSON:	Matt is generally willing to listen to other points of view. For the most

part, he is fair in the means by which he resolves conflicts with his wife, Roxanne. But on certain issues, Matt seems to be an unmovable force. He refuses to listen, refuses to compromise. He insists that he's right on these issues, reminding his wife, "I didn't get to be senior vice president at the bank by not knowing what I was talking about."

Matt is willing to compromise only when it does not cost him anything to do so. And his self-righteous attitude demeans Roxanne. It may seem that Matt's refusal to bend on certain issues doesn't cause that much harm; after all, it isn't as though he is completely inflexible. But his position represents an underlying attitude that he is better or smarter than Roxanne. What would it hurt for him to listen and open his mind to a different point of view? He feels threatened by openness and needs to feel that he is in control in at least a couple of areas. Matt is not only demeaning Roxanne and hurting the relationship, he is also cutting off the opportunity for his own personal growth. Listening, sharing, and compromising are the activities that allow us to be more fully present in our lives and relationships. It is hard to grow when the only sound we hear is the one we are making.

MASK:	The Righteous Accuser
OVERT MESSAGE:	"I have evidence that confirms my worst suspicions about you."
HIDDEN MESSAGE:	"If I trust you, I will become vulnerable."
LESSON:	There is a certain comfort and sense of security in having your negative bi-

ases confirmed. People who are always trying to confirm the worst about another person feel protected by their righteousness. They are masters at uncovering the evidence that supports their suspicions; they always choose the worst-case scenario over giving their partner the benefit of the doubt.

Since going back to work, Louise had been away from home many evenings. Sam had been supportive of Louise's return to work after she had stayed home with their daughter for five years. But, after a while, he felt his support and enthusiasm beginning to wane. He began to question her need to work late so many nights. He could see no good reason for it. Moreover, the more she got into her job and the more nights she worked late, the less interested she seemed to be in sex.

As Sam thought over the events of the past few months, a lot of things seemed to fall into place: the increased number of nights away from home, the decreased interest in sex, Louise's sudden concern with her appearance, and her reduced interest in what was happening to him at work. The more he thought about it, the more convinced he became that Louise was having an affair.

Sam started watching his wife's behavior more carefully, looking for signs that another man was in the picture. And he was finding them, although the signs were ambiguous. Sam prepared for a confrontation, and when it came, it was a disaster.

Louise was furious that Sam suspected her of having an affair. She ticked off the litany of Sam's complaints: "Of course, I'm more interested in how I look. Of course I agree to work later if my boss asks me to. Of course, I'm not always interested in sex when I've had an exhausting day. When you were working hard to get established in your profession, I never accused you of having affairs just because you worked late and were sometimes too tired for sex."

Sam was ashamed of his suspicions. What he had been doing was observing events with a confirmation bias. A confirmation bias means that we seek out evidence primarily to support rather than refute our beliefs or suspicions. Once Sam got the idea in his head that Louise was having an affair, everything he observed seemed to confirm his suspicions.

People who are intent on finding proof for negative assumptions are sometimes just spoiling for a fight. They are the people who make mountains out of molehills, who always blow everything out of proportion. By placing themselves on the offensive, they think they will avoid being the object of attack themselves. They won't allow themselves to become that vulnerable.

MASK: The Pretender

OVERT MESSAGE: "What you don't know won't hurt you."

HIDDEN MESSAGE: "Keeping a part of myself hidden is the only way I can prevent this relationship from taking away all of my freedom."

LESSON: Many people fear that commitment to a relationship implies a loss of freedom. They see themselves helplessly merging with another person until finally there's nothing left of who they once were. Keeping secrets or engaging in deceptions gives them a sense of independence from what they perceive to be the stranglehold of partnership.

Lately, Chuck has started hiding money from his wife, Shelly. Early in their marriage, they made a pact that they would discuss and agree upon all major expenses. For several years, Chuck kept his half of the bargain, even though he was missing out on things he wanted to buy. Later, as he became interested in investing, he found himself missing out on investments he wanted to make because Shelly didn't agree with him. After several years of frustration, Chuck has found a way to cope with what he perceives to be inflexibility on Shelly's part; he goes behind her back. On the surface, he behaves as though he accepts her point of view. But more and more, he just does what he pleases without telling her. The more he does it and gets away with it, the more he is tempted to do it again. Essentially, Chuck leads a double life.

Deception in a relationship can be costly, and one deception tends to lead to another. Eventually, deception spreads like cancer. Chuck's web of lies has become so complex that he can no longer keep track of what he has publicly agreed to with Shelly and what he is trying to hide from her. He now finds that the best strategy is to avoid saying much about anything, lest he trip himself up. Chuck and Shelly need to renegotiate their policy—or what has now become a nonpolicy—of making decisions. Chuck may justify his deceptions as being insignificant in the scheme of things. He may even think that what he is doing is ultimately for Shelly's own good, because he expects his investments to pay off. But once a pattern of deception gets set in a relationship, it tends to spill into other areas. Eventually, Chuck and Shelly will be unable to communicate fully on any issue.

MASK: The Blamer

OVERT MESSAGE: "It's not my problem . . . it's *your* problem."

HIDDEN MESSAGE: "I can't face my own inadequacies, so I blame other people when things aren't working out in my life."

LESSON: Placing blame on others to avoid facing the inadequacies and conflicts in your own life doesn't let you off the hook. In fact, it can be quite costly.

For years, Rodney and Hazel had taken an "us against them" posture, and as a result they had never confronted some serious problems they had. Rodney was a heavy drinker, and sometimes when they attended dinner parties, he would drink too much and get into arguments with other people. On one occasion, the hostess had taken Hazel aside and asked her to take Rodney home because he was embarrassing the guests. Hazel reacted angrily. "How dare you speak that way about Rodney," she said. "What's wrong with you people that you can't take a little fun?" She and Rodney stormed out, complaining all the way home about their uptight hostess and her uptight friends who didn't know how to enjoy themselves.

Rodney and Hazel were like a nation that goes to war in order to stifle internal conflict. In truth, Hazel was often secretly upset when Rodney drank too much, but she was afraid to confront him directly.

Rodney and Hazel's use of displacement to others as a means of pretending to resolve their conflicts gave them a false sense of unity, achieved not through closeness to each other, but through distance and hostility toward others. But their unity was false.

Sometimes, too, when people are struggling within a relationship, they will avoid self-examination by projecting the fears onto a partner. Instead of admitting to personal inadequacies and trying to deal with them, the internal conflict will be externalized.

Jack didn't trust many people, and lately he had reached the conclusion that he couldn't trust his girl friend, Becky, either. Jack frequently went out of town on business, and he started calling Becky two or three times a day, "just to check that everything is okay." Becky wasn't always home when Jack called, and Jack was certain that she was out looking for men. In fact, Becky was not interested in seeing other men, but she was unable to convince Jack of that.

Actually, it was Jack who was looking. Jack's distrust of Becky, as well as his general distrust of other people, was a projection of his own untrustworthiness. When he went out of town, Jack would often go on the prowl. Unable to face the implications of his own unfaithfulness, he transferred it to Becky.

Transferring the blame for your own feelings and actions to your partner will not make you feel better or contribute anything positive to the relationship. Sadly, sometimes a partner will unwittingly participate in the ruse by beginning to believe the criticism.

I once had dinner with a woman colleague and her husband and was dismayed with the way he repeatedly criticized the professional work my colleague had done as an educator. His criticism was without basis; she was a highly respected member of the faculty. In contrast, her stockbroker husband had a pattern of troubles in his career. It occurred to me that he was finding in his wife the inadequacies he could not admit to in himself. Unfortunately, my colleague seemed to believe that her husband's criticism was valid. I questioned her about it later and she admitted that she often wondered about her abilities. Since her self-esteem was low, she had come to believe in the criticism that her husband leveled at her whenever he was struggling with his own career.

Identifying the mask

How do you recognize a mask? Each mask has certain characteristics that provide reliable clues to the underlying message. Some or all of these characteristics will be present when the mask is on. Remember, the masks represent behavior patterns, not types of people. A person might wear more than one mask or a combination of masks. The purpose of this exercise is not to provide you with ammunition against your partner. To say, for example, "You are a pious fraud!" is not particularly useful, and it's not accurate either. Concentrate on recognizing the characteristics, not on placing labels.

THE MASK	COMMON CHARACTERISTICS
The Controller	—Threatens punitive action. —Uses bribery to get his/her way. —Punishes with physical and/or mental abuse. —Belittles a partner's actions, opinions, and feelings. —Makes negative judgments. —Expects to have his/her way.
The Typecaster	—Uses labels to describe others. —Makes value judgments based on superficial data. —Behaves in a condescending or superior way. —Is inflexible. —Makes generalizations.

(Cont.)

THE MASK	COMMON CHARACTERISTICS
The Pious Fraud	—Is full of excuses. —Behaves in a condescending or superior way. —Usually assumes the worst of people. —Often feels victimized by the actions of others. —Always has external justifications to explain his/her behavior. —Can't accept criticism.
The Procrastinator	—Has trouble completing tasks. —Likes to be proved right. —Prefers contracts and protections to agreements based on "good faith." —Hates to plan ahead. —Is always looking for more data. —Can't stand to lose.
The Conflict Avoider	—Rarely shares his/her feelings. —Is secretive and withdrawn. —Hates confrontations. —Thinks people's problems are "all in their head." —Fears intimacy.
The Yes-Sayer	—Is overly agreeable. —Needs frequent assurances that he/she is pleasing others. —Always puts his/her partner's needs first. —Hates arguing. —Expresses little confidence in him/herself.

THE MASK	COMMON CHARACTERISTICS
The Expert	—Usually begins statements with "I." —Tends to dominate conversations. —Makes light of his/her partner's actions, opinions, and feelings. —Always professes to have "the answer." —Feels superior to others. —Brags about his/her achievements. —Feels threatened by others who appear to be knowledgeable.
The Righteous Accuser	—Worries a lot. —Overanalyzes things. —Hates change. —Likes to have proof to back up his/her opinions. —Feels insecure. —Often assumes the worst. —Expresses many prejudices.
The Pretender	—Tends to be quiet and withdrawn. —Agrees to things without taking time to evaluate them. —Behaves defensively when he/she is confronted. —Seems nervous when people try to get close. —Rarely or never shares his/her feelings.
The Blamer	—Often says he/she feels like an outsider. —Thinks people don't understand him/her.

THE MASK	COMMON CHARACTERISTICS
	—Feels superior to others. —Rarely or never admits to being wrong or unable to accomplish a task. —Makes accusations instead of expressing feelings.

Relationship Intelligence is not manipulative. It is not achieving the upper hand in a relationship or learning to "win" through intimidation or deception. These are not smart tactics at all and they will ultimately fail. Relationship Intelligence is seeking solutions in a context of openness and mutual respect. It is being willing to accept compromise and insure that the solutions are taking care of the concerns of both people. Masks get in the way. It's a shame that people sometimes wear them. They're a terrible waste of our individual gifts and precious uniqueness.

CHAPTER NINE

R.I. LESSON SIX

THE MASTER LOVER

There is a story in the Sufi tradition about a man who wanted to sell an old, rough-hewn carpet. He took it to the street and said to the first man who came along, "This is a coarse carpet, which is very worn." The man offered to buy it cheaply, but the carpet seller did not accept his offer. Then, to a second man who passed, he said, "Here is a rare and beautiful carpet. There is none like it." And the man bought the carpet for a high price. A third man, who had observed the transaction, said to the carpet seller, "Please, carpet man, put me in your magic box that can change a worn old carpet into a thing of value."

The greatest challenge of Relationship Intelligence is to find the value in that in which value is not easily seen. Anyone can develop a mastery of the skills needed for Relationship Intelligence, but the skills themselves are only one part of the equation. What makes the task of discovering human love so thrilling and, at the same time, so complex, is its chameleonlike nature. Nothing is ever settled once and for all. We are constantly challenged to transform what is old and worn into something that is new and of great value. For this reason, mastery of Relationship Intelligence requires more than just a knowledge of the techniques. It also requires that you have certain qualities that allow an openness to loving fully. These are not qualities that you are born with; they are qualities that you choose to have. They present the internal context, the window from which you view the things that occur in life. If you do not possess them or have trouble recognizing their value, it is probably because you are still hanging on to some of the myths and false hopes that lead to failure in relationships.

You are limited in your ability to master Relationship Intelligence unless you learn to make these qualities a part of your life:

1. You accept the fact that the future is filled with ambiguity.

2. You look at obstacles and see them as challenges.

3. You embrace the future as a promising opportunity and agree to take reasonable chances, without having a guarantee that things will work out perfectly.

4. You are willing to let go of the things that are interfering with growth and change.

5. You believe in yourself.

6. You can forgive the past mistakes of your partner and remain open to the future.

7. You are able to accept people as they are, and to appreciate the value of human diversity.

8. You act out of your hopes, rather than out of your fears.

9. You are willing to be patient and delay instant gratification for the sake of a long-term good.

10. You treat your partner's concerns as equal to your own.

If you reexamine the examples given in previous chapters, you will always find these qualities either at work or missing. Consider them the foundational points of Relationship Intelligence.

You tolerate ambiguity

Relationships are inherently ambiguous. Much of the time, it is hard to pinpoint exactly what is going on. Some people are willing to accept ambiguity as a given in a relationship and work to improve communication to reduce its negative consequences. But for others, ambiguity is a constant source of frustration and unhappiness.

Reuben and Dora are out celebrating. It is the biggest celebration they have had in five years. They are eating at one of the fanciest restaurants in the city and spending a lot of money on the celebration. But one thing they are not spending money on is alcohol. They are both drinking coffee with their scrumptious dinner. What are Reuben and Dora celebrating? They're celebrating what in this book has been called "problem recognition." Two months earlier, Reuben attended his first meeting of Alcoholics Anonymous and admitted to the people there and, most important, to himself that he was an alcoholic.

The problem of Reuben's alcoholism isn't solved, and Reuben and Dora have a lot of work to do before they'll be able to heal the damage Reuben's drinking has done to their marriage.

For five years, Dora lived with broken promises and verbally abusive behavior. She lived with the hope that eventually things would change, that Reuben would keep his promise to stop drinking. But even when things improved, the improvements never lasted for long. She continued to harbor the hope that the day would come when Reuben would recognize his problem and do something about it. But she was always on guard.

Finally, a friend introduced her to Al Anon, a support organization for people involved with alcoholics. At the meeting, she encountered other people who were in the same situation. She learned how to stop blaming herself for Reuben's drinking, and also to recognize that ultimately Reuben had to take responsibility for himself. And, after Dora had been attending Al Anon meetings for a year, Reuben finally did face his problem. It happened after his boss threatened to fire him unless he got help for his drinking.

On the evening Reuben and Dora celebrated, Reuben had not had a drink for two months. Their lives and their marriage had improved dramatically, but the situation was not without ambiguity. Dora knew that in living with a recovering alcoholic, her life would never be without that ambiguity. But she was willing to accept it as a part of her life and, along with Reuben, take things one day at a time.

Reuben and Dora's marriage may hold more ambiguity than some, but ambiguity is present in every relationship. We cannot always control our lives or our environment. The ability to understand and accept the uncertainties of the future is an important quality of Relationship Intelligence.

In the first blush of love, we make promises, and mean them. We say, "I'll never leave you," "I'll never hurt you," "I'll always feel this way about you." We try, with our words and our wills, to pin down the future, in the same way that the Three Little Pigs sealed their house against the wolf's attack. But there is no way to be absolutely secure in life. People who are successful at love accept ambiguity. More than that, they are able to rejoice in the mysterious turns of life.

You see obstacles as challenges

Sooner or later, every relationship runs into obstacles. They might be financial, parental, career-related, sexual, or any number of things. People who thrive in relationships are those who are willing to accept obstacles as challenges rather than as signs of defeat.

Unless you accept obstacles as part of the challenge of a relationship, it is unlikely that you will be very successful. Moreover, your ability to overcome difficulties will be greatly enhanced if your partner feels the same way. It is much easier to get over the rough spots if both of you strive to do so, rather than if one of you carries all the burden. If one of you carries the burden, you may force change occasionally, but it probably won't work over the long term. When you both contribute, you can usually overcome your problems. Indeed, this is one of the cornerstones of a good relationship.

June and Vern have a problem they have lived with for six years. Their son, Danny, is autistic. From very early on, they recognized that Danny had some kind of problem, but it took the doctors a while to diagnose it. At first, they thought it might just be slightly slow development. Then the possibility of mental retardation was raised. Eventually, a child psychiatrist had diagnosed Danny as autistic. He is now in a special school that attempts to treat autism with behavior modification. June and Vern have refused to have Danny treated with drugs.

Danny's autism has placed a tremendous strain on his parents' relationship. Every day, there seems to be a fresh set of obstacles to confront. Some days, June and Vern experience hope, only to have their hope dashed. They have no idea what will happen to their son over the long term. Sometimes they don't even know whether they will make it through together over the long term. They live day-to-day, trying to keep things together and trying to cope with the enormous emotional, intellectual, and financial drain they are experiencing.

Sometimes June and Vern ask themselves how they manage to overcome the daily obstacles that are thrown in their path. There are no easy answers. Both of them love Danny dearly, and yet both would admit that there are times when they resent him profoundly for what he has done to their lives. They know that Danny's problems are not his fault, but nevertheless they find themselves longing for a normal, peaceful life.

Ultimately, they have decided that what has seen them through is their commitment. They made a deal to stay together, for better or for worse. Even when things are worse, they stick to the deal. They made a commitment to raise their child, never expecting it to entail such great struggle. They were wrong. But they feel a responsibility to honor their commitment. They view their son's problem as a challenge the entire family is responsible for confronting, rather than as an impossible impediment to their success as a family. In many ways, they have found that their shared struggle has brought them closer together and enriched their lives in countless ways.

Viewing your problems as challenges is not a stoic posture. It doesn't mean "grin and bear it." Rather, it is having a deep curiosity about life, a tendency to ask, when problems arise, "What is this teaching me? How can I turn this problem into something of value?"

You embrace the future

"Nothing ventured, nothing gained," goes the old saying. People who succeed in relationships are those who are willing to try new things. They are not afraid to open themselves up to the possibilities that the future offers. If you remain stuck in the present, with an eye to the past, you may never get hurt—at least, not in the way you have learned to think about hurt. But you'll never be where the action in life is, either.

Embracing the future does not mean that you behave like a stuntman, crashing against life at every turn. Being a thrill-seeker won't help you achieve a mastery of love. The challenge is not to seek out risks, but rather to accept them when they present themselves.

José is at a crisis point in his life. After a messy divorce, he turned shy of marriage and has been playing the field for ten years. But for the past year, he has been more or less steadily dating Carmen, a real departure from his usual pattern. He has been happy with her and hasn't had a desire to play the field. But he has also been reluctant to commit to more than a dating relationship with her. Now Carmen wants something more. She has confronted José about his unwillingness to commit. On the one hand, José feels as though he is being pushed. On the other hand, he understands Carmen's position. He knows that, after a year, she is within her rights to want more of a commitment. He feels that the relationship is quite a good one, although not without its flaws. The question is whether he should take the risk and give Carmen a higher level of commitment.

Carmen gently points out to José that, although he doesn't feel "ready" for a commitment, his real fear is of the risk that is present in any relationship. She suggests that he'll never feel 100 percent ready, and that, if he hopes to ever have a good relationship, he's going to have to be willing to accept a certain amount of risk. Carmen's remarks strike a chord in José. He begins to think about the risk he would be taking were he to make a serious commitment. He decides that having Carmen in his life is worth the risk. He does not want to lose her and spend his life wondering if he passed up an opportunity of great value.

Once José decides to make a commitment, he feels as though a great burden has been lifted from his shoulders. He has an insight: The future is what life is all about. By choosing to move his life into the future, José has scored a victory over his fears.

You seek growth

Truly creative people are always growing. They understand that life is a dynamic process and that to stand still is to stagnate. The myth of living "happily ever after" denies the necessity of growth and change. Life is not like that, and neither are relationships. Relationships require ongoing renewal, and sometimes they change in major ways. Successful couples are not afraid to change and grow.

There is always the danger in a relationship that you might grow apart. When you first meet someone, you may find that you are compatible and that you get along well because you are at a point in your lives when your needs are closely matched. But it's possible that the person who attracts you now may not have attracted you at another time in your life when your mutual needs were not as similar. It is important to realize that the closeness you feel now may not continue or be easily maintained. The most difficult task in a relationship is often being able to grow together rather than apart. To accomplish this, you need to put as much communication, support, and sharing into your relationship as possible.

Von likes to talk about how unfairly life has treated him. He feels that he has had a string of bad breaks. In his neighborhood, he grew up on the "wrong side of the tracks," so other children, and especially teachers, never gave him very much respect. His parents could not afford to provide him with the things he saw his classmates getting. When he was twelve, his father left home and never made any further effort to contact Von. Von's grades in school were decent, but not quite high enough to get him into the state university system, so he ended up attending junior college. His grades at the junior college were just below what he would have needed to transfer to a good university. When it came time to find a job, he had some bad breaks in interviewing, and was unable to get the job he wanted. Once women hear about Von's bad breaks—his first and favorite story to tell—they, too, fail to give him the respect he feels he merits. As a result, none of his relationships ever progress beyond the first couple of dates.

Von is a good example of someone who is stuck in an old story. He believes he wants to get ahead in life. He believes he wants to establish a permanent relationship with a woman. But he is unwilling to grow. The past forms a barrier between Von and the open possibilities of the future. He cannot accept responsibility for his past mistakes—they "happened" to him; they were "bad breaks"—so his life remains on hold.

Von might initially attract someone who, like him, feels taken advantage of by life. But the relationship would be doomed from the start. Either she would outgrow him and move on, or they would both use the past as an excuse for the problems in the relationship and it would be mired in negativity.

The willingness to grow and take responsibility for one's life is a fundamental quality of a successful relationship. Furthermore, this quality is essential to the ability to live productively. When we allow ourselves to be stuck in a negative self-story, we do not take advantage of the gift of life.

You believe in yourself

There will be many times, during the course of a relationship, when you will find yourself questioning your judgment, possibly even your sanity. There may be times when you begin to lose belief in yourself and begin to doubt that you have made the right decisions. Indeed, it is impossible to be involved in a close relationship without making mistakes. But one of the most important lessons about intelligence is that smart people are not people who never make mistakes; they are people who learn something of value from their mistakes. The ultimate test of Relationship Intelligence is how much you learn from your mistakes and how well you apply what you learn.

An important skill to develop is the ability to detach yourself from your mistakes and view them objectively. Ultimately, you are the person you are, not only because of your successes, but also because of your failures. But whether you succeed or fail, you need to keep the courage of your convictions and your belief in yourself. If you don't believe in yourself, you can't expect anyone else to believe in you.

Ben was a paraplegic as the result of an automobile accident that happened when he was in his mid-twenties. Before the accident, Ben was athletic, active, vibrant, and as alive as anyone could be. He and his wife, Mary, had what many of their friends considered to be a storybook romance. They felt invulnerable, as though they could achieve anything in life.

The accident changed all that, at least for a while. Ben went through a severe depression; then his depression turned to anger. He had had everything in life to look forward to, and now he felt he had nothing. He brooded bitterly about the unfairness of his plight. But Ben had two powerful things going for him. The first was that, deep down, he believed in himself. The second was that Mary believed in him, too. Within a year of the accident, Ben had pulled himself through his depression and anger. His work in advertising, which had always been creative, became even more so, and he was rapidly promoted in his firm. His relationship with Mary grew more intimate as a result of their shared struggle. Ben realized that he still had a lot to get out of life, and a lot to give to it. He found ways around his handicap and tried to make the most of his situation. It was possible because his belief in himself made others believe in him, too.

The secret of Ben's success was his ability to sepa-

rate his lifeless legs from who he was as a human being. His legs did not define him; they did not make him
more or less creative. Ben could see that his strengths
as a human being existed beyond his wheelchair. It was
a courageous conclusion, and ultimately, one that
would enhance his life and his relationships with others.

You are willing to forgive

I know people who pride themselves on never forget-
ting or forgiving a slight. They possess photographic
memories for what they perceive to be insults or
wrongs, and they are willing to wait months, sometimes
years, to get their revenge. Or they "get back" in more
passive ways, reminding the person who hurt them of
the past behavior. As a result, they continue, year after
year, to throw hand grenades into the relationship.

Howie and Dot have a good marriage. It might even
be a great one, were it not for Dot's long memory and
the way she uses it. She keeps a running catalog of
everything Howie has done wrong, and she knows just
when to bring up reminders of his past behavior. She
does this in order to keep Howie in his place, but the
effect is to reduce the intimacy between them. Howie
holds back, afraid of having the past thrown in his face.

Since all of us make mistakes and do things we are
not proud of, forgiveness is a central dynamic in a successful relationship. We need to ask ourselves: What is
the value to holding on to our past grievances? What is
achieved by getting even? Many people are fearful of
looking like "wimps" if they don't get even for past
slights. They worry that turning the other cheek will
only lead people to walk all over them. But, in fact, the
quality of being able to forgive is the true sign of

strength. Forgiveness opens the door to positive change; seeking revenge closes it.

Dot's constant harping on his past mistakes has made Howie cynical. He no longer listens to her when she begins to criticize him. The reason he doesn't listen is because there is no respect for him in her criticism. Nor is there any commitment to resolving their problems.

If you find that you are struggling to forgive your partner for a past mistake, you should examine what your end goal is. Are you interested in finding a way to make your relationship better, or are you more interested in punishing your partner and making him or her suffer? Your answer to this question will determine whether you will be open to resolving your conflicts and growing in your relationship.

You can accept others as they are

Most people have at least some desire to exert control over others. We imagine what we would like other people to be, and then, consciously or unconsciously, we try to mold them into the image we have created. Some of the changes for which we work may be genuinely constructive. But too often we ask others to be what they are not. Sometimes people fall in love with an image, not the reality, and spend their relationships resenting that their partners cannot be what they never were.

You are never going to find anyone who is the perfect image of what you are looking for. So find someone whose perceived flaws are ones you can live with and accept them, just as you hope that person will accept your flaws. This is not to say that you should never try to help a person improve. But you must understand that improvement can't be forced from the outside; it must come from within.

Sarah is like so many of us who believe, in principle, that others should be allowed to be themselves. But she has very well-defined ideas of what she expects from others, and when they don't conform to those ideas, sooner or later she tries to get them to change. She fell in love with Jim, a musician, but she was never pleased with his unsettled life-style. She wanted him to settle down and work a regular job, and she couldn't accept the person Jim was. The early years of their marriage were stormy, as Jim continued to pursue his music and Sarah continued to push him to find a more stable career. One might ask: With whom did Sarah fall in love? It wasn't Jim, as he was. It was Jim as she wanted and wished him to be. She did not love the real Jim.

Sometimes the thrill of romance can dazzle us to the point where we put off confronting the truth about a person. We avoid examining real issues, such as: Is this a person whose goals and life-style match what we want in life? A decision to commit to another person is also a decision to accept that person for what he or she is.

You are optimistic

A bottle half empty is also a bottle half full. How you describe it has to do with your inner sense of optimism. It is a lot easier, and generally more satisfying, to live with a person who sees the bottle half full than one who sees it half empty. Almost any turn of events can be construed in a way that is either more positive or more negative. If you turn every disagreement into a major crisis and every misfortune into a major disaster, or if you look for the downside of every happy event, you will succeed not only in making yourself miserable, but in doing the same for those around you.

Francine is a master at pulling defeat from the jaws of victory. No matter what happens, she can find a reason to criticize. When she and Kenneth bought a new car, she predicted that the car would turn out to be a lemon. Whenever anything went wrong with the car, which wasn't that often, she delighted in reminding Kenneth of her earlier predictions. When Kenneth worked hard and got a 10 percent raise, she was quick to ask why he didn't get more. When her children brought home good grades, she chided them that the grades could have been better.

Francine might argue that she was just being realistic, that she didn't believe in "pie in the sky." But there is a difference between being realistic about the ups and downs of life and seeking out the downside.

Some people wait for happiness to come to them, expecting it to appear as a bolt out of the blue. They do not seek it out, nor do they recognize it in the life they have. If you do not possess the quality of optimism, it will be hard for you to truly succeed in a relationship. Relationships constantly demand that we operate from our hopes, not our fears. They challenge us to find the possibilities in every struggle. If you're predisposed to look on the gloomy side, even the everyday hassles of being in a relationship might feel overwhelming.

You have patience

When things aren't going our way, we often need patience to allow time for them to work themselves out. We do not live in an age when people are very good at delaying gratification. But sometimes we would be much happier if we were willing to wait for gratification, rather than insisting on having everything right away.

In matters of love, we are especially reluctant to let time take its course. We cannot stand to be without a mate and when we find someone we like, we want to rush into commitment. There is a sense of desperation underlying our search for love, a fear that we might miss out on it altogether and be lonely forever.

After her divorce, Anna was desperate to find another man. She was approaching forty and she believed that her time was running out. Soon she would be too old to attract anyone. She rushed into several relationships and they all turned out badly. In trying too hard to make things happen fast, Anna was driving men away. Finally, she became so discouraged that she stopped trying to initiate relationships. She began to focus more on herself and on her interests. She joined a political organization and began to make new friends. Over time, she found that she was feeling better about herself and more hopeful about her future. She had little time to feel lonely and when she thought about having a relationship, she realized that she no longer felt such a sense of panic.

Two years after she joined the political organization, she began to date a man she had met at a meeting. The early focus of their relationship was on their common work, rather than on a sense of need. Eventually, their feelings for one another grew deeper. But neither of them felt they had to force the relationship. They let it happen naturally. Successful relationships are not born from desperation. Nor do they happen overnight. It takes time to develop the bond of intimacy that is needed to make a relationship strong and enduring. The term "love at first sight" would be better phrased as "passion at first sight." And the urgency of passion is not a sufficient foundation for a lasting relationship.

Your love is selfless

If I were asked the single most frequent cause of the destruction of relationships, and the single biggest contributor to "dumb love," I would say it is selfishness. We live in an age of narcissism and many people have never learned or have forgotten how to listen to the needs of others. The truth is, if you want to make just one change in yourself that will improve your relationship—literally, overnight—it would be to put your partner's interests on an equal footing with your own. Selflessness does not mean that you sacrifice your own wants and needs for another person's. Rather, it is the ability to achieve a balance in your relationship. You respect your partner and consider his or her needs as being just as important as yours. And you possess the quality of compassion—the ability to recognize and respond during those times when your partner needs more attention than you do.

Rex and Julia are among the two or three happiest couples I've met. I've talked with both of them at some length, seeking the secret of their success. They don't believe they have any secret, except perhaps that they work hard at their relationship. But I've noticed something special about them: They are truly equals. When their needs are in conflict, neither of them assumes that the other person's point is more important. Their respect for each other was demonstrated most clearly in the way they handled their careers. Eight years ago, Rex, who is a medical researcher, had an opportunity to work on an important project in another state. They discussed the move at some length, and Julia, a lawyer, decided that she was willing to leave her job because it was such an important opportunity for Rex. Then, five years later, Julia received an attractive job offer in another city. Once again, they discussed the implications of a move. This time, Rex agreed to move. He was well enough established at that point that he was sure he could find a position in the new city. As he explained it, "Julia has made sacrifices and moved for me. It's my turn to make sacrifices for her."

Selfishness is usually based in a fear people have that, once they open the door, they will be swept away by a violent tide and soon lose all of their freedom and individuality. On the other hand, I have observed people who *always* put others' needs ahead of their own, claiming that their needs are not worthy of equal consideration. The concept of equality transcends both of these responses. The quality of selflessness allows two people to be everything they can be as individuals, while they grow as a couple.

Change occurs incrementally, not overnight. Few people who read these words are going to say, "Ah, now I know where I've gone wrong," and emerge tomorrow as entirely different people. But if you are struggling with a current relationship or finding that all of your relationships eventually come unglued, you might want to consider whether you lack any of the fundamental relationship qualities. Take this quiz and find out.

——————————— **QUIZ** ———————————

Love Mastery—Do You Have the Right Stuff?

Instructions: Answer "true" or "false" to the following statements.

1. You like to know in advance what is going to happen in your relationship. _____T _____F

2. You aren't satisfied unless you have frequent evidence that your relationship is going well. _____T _____F

3. You can accept the fact that relationships are filled with mystery. _____T _____F

4. You are often fearful that your relationship won't last. _____T _____F

5. There are certain obstacles that you know you could never overcome in a relationship. _____T _____F

6. You actively work to make your relationship better, no matter what problems you encounter. _____T _____F

7. You don't consider yourself a quitter. _____T _____F

8. When things go wrong, you feel bitter, because you think you deserve better. _____T _____F

9. It's okay to take risks early in a relationship, but you shouldn't have to after a certain point. _____T _____F

10. Since nothing is certain, you are always prepared for the worst to happen. _____T _____F

11. There is always a certain amount of risk involved in opening yourself up to another person. _____T _____F

12. You are afraid that either you or your partner will change and become less satisfied with the relationship. _____T _____F

13. It is natural for people to change and feel less intimate as time goes on. _____T _____F

14. You believe that a certain amount of change is necessary —and good—in life and in relationships. _____T _____F

15. You are basically confident that you will find a way to handle the ups and downs of life. _____T _____F

16. There are some actions that you could never forgive. _____T _____F

17. If you don't respond aggressively to certain behavior, you think that people will walk all over you. _____T _____F

18. You'd rather get on with your life than waste time holding grudges. _____T _____F

19. If you see qualities in your partner that you think are negative, you try to change them. _____T _____F

20. You enjoy the differences among people. _____T _____F

21. You are generally optimistic. _____T _____F

22. You tend to be critical when you see that other people are not living up to their potential. _____T _____F

23. When things are going well in your life, you are always expecting something to go wrong. _____T _____F

24. You hate to wait for what you want. _____T _____F

25. You are miserable if things are not going the way you want them to in a relationship. _____T _____F

26. Sometimes the best way to respond to a problem is to do and say nothing. _____T _____F

27. Your partner's needs are as important as your own. _____T _____F

28. You believe that if you don't look out for yourself, no one will. _____T _____F

29. You can't fully give yourself to another person without losing something of yourself. _____T _____F

Scoring:

Add 5 points for each of the "true" answers you gave for the following statements:

_____ 3	_____ 14	_____ 22
_____ 6	_____ 15	_____ 27
_____ 7	_____ 18	_____ 28
_____ 11	_____ 21	_____ Total

Subtract 1 point for each of the "true" answers you gave for the following statements:

_____ 1	_____ 12	_____ 24
_____ 2	_____ 13	_____ 25
_____ 4	_____ 16	_____ 26
_____ 5	_____ 17	_____ 29
_____ 8	_____ 19	_____ Total
_____ 9	_____ 20	
_____ 10	_____ 23	

Subtract your second total from the first. This is your score.

If you scored between 35 and 55 points, you have internalized many of the attitudes necessary for success in relationships. A score of between 20 and 35 shows that, while you have reached a positive point in some of your understandings about life and relationships, you are still struggling to come to terms with issues that are holding you back. If you scored below 20, you probably experience a constant struggle in your relationships and usually find them threatening and unsatisfying.

If you lack the qualities that are the basis of love mastery, there is no secret method for learning them. But your acknowledgment of their importance and your will to achieve them is an important first step. Maybe the next time you feel despair over your relationship, you will stop and ask, "What is the challenge here?" Or the next time you are filled with fear about a proposed change, you will decide to take a risk. One step at a time, you can choose to allow the qualities of the master lover to emerge and become an integral part of the way you think and behave.

CHAPTER TEN

QUESTIONS AND ANSWERS ABOUT RELATIONSHIP INTELLIGENCE

❖

When I give lectures or conduct research, people often ask questions about the idea of Relationship Intelligence. I've noticed that certain questions occur more often than others; these are the areas where people seem to struggle most intensely.

You encourage people to check their perceptions, but when I'm in love, I don't really know what they are. In fact, I feel confused.

When you say you are confused, you are really expressing one of several things: (1) You don't have the information you need to make a decision; (2) You aren't willing to make a decision; or (3) You don't trust or accept your perceptions.

Confusion is not a valid state in itself, although many people think the appropriate response to confusion is to wait for a light to go on in their heads. Confusion always implies that some action should be taken. If information is missing, go after it. For example, you may say you're confused because you are missing some input from your partner, such as whether or not he or she is committed to the relationship. Or your confusion might be a sign that you are hesitating to risk a commitment, either for valid reasons (which you should examine) or because you're afraid to enter into a commitment that is, by nature, ambiguous.

Maybe you don't trust your perceptions because there's a gap between what you want and what you think will work. You might be saying, "I know this person isn't good for me, but I love him so much." If this is the case, you are abiding by a romantic myth that love is equated primarily with your feelings for a person. Examine the balance of passion, intimacy, and commitment in your relationship. This will help you evaluate whether it has true potential over the long term.

Do we only repeat the maladaptive schemas from the past? Couldn't chemistry tie in with the "healthy" schemas?

Of course, many past schemas are not maladaptive. And we carry these with us into adulthood, as we do the maladaptive schemas. But research indicates that this thing we call "chemistry" often brings the maladaptive schemas to the surface. All this means is that we should not idealize chemistry as being an unpredictable, crazy aspect of love. And we should not trust the chemistry we experience with another person to tell us whether that person will make a good partner.

I believe that my husband should be the closest person in my life, and I feel as though I'm betraying him when I confide things to my friends that I haven't told him.

If you can't share things with your husband, and your marriage does not have the bonded aspect we call intimacy, you have a valid concern. You need to deal directly with your husband to find out what is lacking, rather than looking for others to provide the closeness that is missing in your marriage.

On the other hand, it is natural, and even healthy, for us to be close to other people than our romantic partners. You may appreciate qualities in a friend that your husband doesn't have, but that does not mean that your husband is lacking.

In general, couples are probably too threatened by the important people in their partners' lives. A successful partnership thrives in the presence of close friendships and family. These other relationships don't necessarily detract from the partnership.

My boyfriend is not a talker, so, even if I observe his nonverbal signals, how do I know what they mean?

If you know him well, you can probably make certain assumptions about the signals, based on past behavior. You may have to take a different approach to encourage him to share with you. For example, instead of saying, "What's wrong?" to which he may reply, "Nothing," say, "I've noticed that, in the past, when you've been concerned about money, you've behaved this way. Why don't we talk about it?" This might force a more open response. If it doesn't, and if your boyfriend generally refuses to share his thoughts and feelings, you need to ask yourself whether you can really have a satisfying relationship with him. What is missing is intimacy, a key component of a strong partnership.

Does an "intelligent" person have a better chance of being relationship-intelligent?

In *The Triarchic Mind,* I defined intelligence as having three components: (1) the ability to reason; (2) common sense, or the ability to make practical judgments; and (3) insight, or the ability to think creatively. Your mastery of these three components might make you more open to the concept of Relationship Intelligence. For example, if you always apply rigid criteria to every arena of your life, you will probably tend to do it in relationships, too. Or if you tend to look for creative ways of handling things, rather than depending on standard approaches, it's likely you'll do the same in relationships.

But there are two cautions. The first is that Relationship Intelligence implies certain assumptions that are not necessarily true for intelligence in general. There's a particular context that includes other dynamics such as empathy, compassion, intuition, and passion. You might be creative, but without empathy, your creativity will be meaningless.

Second, Relationship Intelligence is always interactive. It requires the element of commitment to making something happen in cooperation with another person or persons. Therefore, even if your reasoning skills are strong, they will not necessarily lead you to a solution. In fact, sometimes reasoning skills get in the way.

Are you saying that, in an ideal relationship, the three components of intimacy, passion, and commitment will be balanced?

Nothing in life is ever completely balanced. The components of intimacy, passion, and commitment will constantly move in a relationship, taking on different weights at different times. But in a long-term romantic relationship, the partners will be aware of the importance of developing all three components and will strive to do so. An understanding of the significance of the love triangle will also help couples evaluate the state of their relationship at any given point and to make diagnoses about what might be needed. It will help them keep things in perspective. For example, a lessening of passion at one point in a relationship will not lead to the generalized conclusion that everything about the relationship is at risk.

I know I choose the wrong types of men. They always have some kind of problem—like alcohol, or they're married, or they don't have a job. But these are the people I'm most attracted to.

You are describing a chemistry that is probably based on past problems and insecurities. The most important thing for you to know is that you are not helpless to change your destructive attractions. What are these relationships providing that you think you need or want? Do you think your needs are valid (growth-promoting) or invalid (fear-based)? Is your evaluation of your needs centered on romantic myths? One thing that stands out as being consistent among all the examples you gave is that these men are especially needy. What might your tendency to be attracted to needy or poorly functioning men say about your own self-story? Are you afraid that you can't measure up to or aren't worthy of a relationship with someone who is strong? Do you think that a partner's neediness is the only reason he has to stay with you?

There are many possible reasons for your destructive attractions. You can start to deal with your tendency to be attracted to impossible partnerships only when you start believing that you have the skills to evaluate and take action. No person is a victim of love.

I've tried everything I can think of to solve the problems in my marriage, and I feel like I'm wasting my time. How do I know when it's time to leave?

There is no single "rule" for making a decision like this. But there are some steps you can take to evaluate your situation. Now that you know more about the nature of problem solving in relationships, you can first ask yourself if you have tried using the procedures described in this book to solve your problems. For example, have you identified your problems accurately, checking your own and your partner's perceptions? Have you looked for places that your romantic ideals have been getting in the way? Have you solicited help from the outside when it has been necessary? Have you made a commitment to change?

There may be things at work in your relationship

that prevent resolution. For example, if your partner refuses to listen to you, treats you with disrespect, or even abuses you, there may be nothing you can do to make a change. Problem solving in relationships must start from a point where both partners are willing to work together with love and respect. If the fundamental qualities of love and respect are absent, you cannot force them to be there.

I don't expect this book to give you all the answers and tell you what you should definitely do. You take a risk, whether you go or stay. But the precepts of Relationship Intelligence can at least give you a basis for beginning to evaluate your true situation so you can take action.

My husband and I will talk over a problem, and it will seem to be solved, but then nothing really changes. I'm getting frustrated. How do I know if something has really been dealt with?

Chances are, you are leaving out the action steps in the problem-solving technique. You both agree that you want to make a change, but you don't follow up your intention by deciding what will be done. If you say that, in the future, you're going to share household work more equally, but don't distribute specific tasks and provide for accountability, your good intentions will never be realized. Or if you decide something vague like you're going to "talk more," but you don't specify what that means, any change will probably be temporary. It is not enough to be in agreement about a solution. You must also commit your resources, decide on the actions required, and determine a method for monitoring your progress.

You say that selflessness is an important quality, but as far as I'm concerned, my main problem is that I'm selfless. When I'm with a man, I always put him first, and I can't shake the feeling that I should give him what he wants. I know this isn't healthy. How can I change it?

The quality of selflessness implies that there is equality in the relationship; each person's concerns are given equal weight. There are times when one person's needs are going to be a priority. But if you always give in, at the expense of your own needs, that is not selflessness. Don't you think you deserve the same amount of respect as your partner?

Your problem-solving method makes a lot of sense, but I can't see my husband agreeing to sit down and go through it.

Problem solving doesn't always occur in a structured way. You solve dozens of problems informally every day. However, if you and your husband have reached a roadblock, and the issue is serious, an informal conversation probably won't be enough. You don't have to follow the step-by-step procedure I outlined in Chapter Five. But keep a mental checklist handy: How does each of you perceive the problem? How can you articulate the problem together in a challenge statement (what would have to happen for the problem to be handled)? What options are available? What actions are you going to take?

My wife is overly emotional. I think that sometimes using formal logic would help us to objectify our problems.

Formal logic does not help objectify relationship problems. Logic starts with a statement of fact, and the facts are more elusive when it comes to real-life problems, because what is true for you might not be true for your wife. What you might be saying is that your wife, because she is emotional, does not know the facts, but you, because you are not emotional, do. That assumption might be valid in the classroom or on the job, but it is not valid in relationships.

It's okay to be emotional. Our emotions, like our words and actions, are expressions of what is really occurring for us. Of course, emotions aren't enough. But you might want to examine why your wife has a problem moving beyond her emotional response. It may be that, in the past, when she tried to express her feelings more straightforwardly, her "logical" husband shot her down. Are you really listening to her?

If intimacy and commitment are there, but not passion, should we assume that passion just isn't there, or can it come later?

Most of the time, an initial attraction, which includes feelings of passion, is the first thing we experience in a romantic relationship. Intimacy and the decision to commit take longer. But this isn't always true, because passion also implies an emotional response that is closely linked to intimacy. You might achieve intimacy with a person and, as it deepens, it will spark a new emotional response that generates passion. Most people think of sexual attraction as a purely physical, and very mysterious, occurrence. But it is more complex than that. Sexual attraction is intricately linked with our ideas, emotions, and values—and all of these are subject to change. To use a simple example: Let's say you think that a certain type of person is sexually attractive, but another type is not. The mental criteria you have established are going to influence your physical response. But what if you then meet someone who does not fit your criteria, but for whom you feel a strong attachment? Your mental criteria might change to include the new data.

Whenever my husband and I have a fight, we always end up in bed, and nothing really gets resolved.

That's because you fight. Fighting sets up an emotionally charged arena. It's passionate. So it makes sense that you extend your passion and respond sexually. But fighting is not necessarily related to problem solving. It's a system of offensive–offensive or offensive–defensive behavior. Problem solving is characterized by cooperative behavior.

Expressions of anger or sorrow or frustration might occur when you begin to address a problem. But if you never move beyond the passion, you're not committed to a solution.

My problem isn't anything specific. I just don't feel the same love for my wife that I once did.

Every problem can be grounded in specifics, even if it seems, at first, to be vague and undefined. Sometimes you have to be the detective of your own feelings, and ask yourself why they might be occurring. For example, do you experience less intimacy than you once did? Do you spend less time together? Have your values or your partner's values changed? Or has one of you developed interests that the other does not share? Are you angry about something you haven't been able to articulate? Were your original ideas about the way a relationship should be based on myths that are not true? There are many questions you can ask that will provide clues to what your feelings are telling you. Once you've identified the specific things with which you're struggling, you can then take steps to identify what must be done to reach a resolution.

Are you saying that all relationship problems can be solved?

If you think of a problem as being a challenge, you can conclude that every problem can be resolved. But you have to be willing to accept that the results might not be what you anticipated or even wanted. Sometimes, the resolution of a relationship problem means ending the relationship. You must also be open to the idea that life's problems, or challenges, are not static. They are unlike academic problems that can be solved once and for all. The way you resolve a life problem takes you to a different point, where a new challenge is waiting to be addressed. As humans, we have endless problems, and therefore, endless opportunities for growth and discovery.

RECOMMENDED
READING

❖

Brehm, S. S. *Intimate Relationships*. New York: Random House, 1985.

This book contains a fairly comprehensive survey of the state of our knowledge about intimate relationships. It covers a broad range of topics, such as physical attraction, liking, loving, and relationship patterns. It is written in the form of a textbook, but is easily accessible to a lay reader.

Gardner, H. *Frames of Mind: The Theory of Multiple Intelligences*. New York: Basic Books, 1983.

Howard Gardner's theory of multiple intelligences, which goes beyond conventional views about assessing mental capacities, is explored. Two of the intelligences outlined by Gardner are intrapersonal and interpersonal.

Sternberg, R. J., and Barnes, M. L., eds. *The Psychology of Love*. New Haven, CT: Yale University Press, 1988.

This book contains sixteen essays by leading theorists and researchers in the field of love. The essays are written in an easy-to-read style. Although the authors express disagreement on many points, the controversies provide lively and provocative reading about the nature of love.

Sternberg, R. J. *The Triangle of Love*. New York: Basic Books, 1988.

This book presents a complete exposition of my triangular theory of love and of the research conducted by myself and others that supports this theory. It also considers related topics, such as the nature and typical stages of interpersonal relationships.

Sternberg, R. J. *The Triarchic Mind*. New York: Viking, 1988.

In this book, I present a full exposition of my triarchic theory of human intelligence, and describe how it applies in both school and work-related settings. This book, written for lay audiences, also contains exercises that can be useful in increasing one's intellectual skills.

Sternberg, R. J., and Wagner, R. K., eds. *Practical Intelligence: Nature and Origins of Competence in the Everyday World*. New York: Cambridge University Press, 1986.

This book contains a series of essays by distinguished leaders in the field of practical intelligence on how intelligence can be applied to everyday life. It will be useful to those who want to understand the use of intelligence in a variety of life arenas.

ABOUT THE AUTHORS

Robert J. Sternberg is IBM Professor of Psychology and Education at Yale University and the author of several books, including *The Triarchic Mind—A New Theory of Human Intelligence* and *The Triangle of Love*. He is the recipient of numerous grants and awards, including a John Simon Guggenheim Fellowship. He was named one of the top 100 "Young Scientists in the U.S." by *Science Digest* and was listed in the 1986 *Esquire* magazine register of "Outstanding Men and Women Under 40." He lives in Mt. Carmel, Connecticut.

Catherine Whitney is the author of *Uncommon Lives—Gay Men & Straight Women* and has collaborated on several other books in the human relations field, including *Born to Please—Compliant Women, Controlling Men* and *Love and Anger: The Parental Dilemma*. She is currently at work on a book about abortion. Ms. Whitney lives in New York City.